Laughter From
The Hills

God bless you,
Alyce Faye Bragg

Laughter From The Hills

Alyce Faye Bragg

Charleston, West Virginia

Quarrier Press
Charleston, WV

Book and cover design: Mark S. Phillips

ISBN 13: 978-1-891852-64-0
ISBN 10: 1-891852-64-7

Library of Congress Catalog Card Number: 2009931647

10 9 8 7 6 5 4 3 2 1

Printed in the United States of America

Distributed by:

West Virginia Book Company
1125 Central Ave.
Charleston, WV 25302
www.wvbookco.com

Dedicated to my wonderful family—
without them there would be no stories.

Contents

Prologue

Laughter is a gift from God. When He created us, He must have realized that we needed an ingredient to balance our lives, so He installed a sense of humor—in most of us anyway. A sense of humor can defuse a volatile situation, bring ease to an embarrassing moment, and promote a healthy outlook.

A good hearty laugh is healthy. The Bible tells us "A merry heart doeth good like a medicine," and goes on to say, "But a broken spirit drieth the bones." I dislike being around someone whose bones have dried, and the juices of their laughter have withered. Not only are they despondent and pessimistic, but also their attitude affects everyone else around them. Even in tense, serious situations, someone with an optimistic attitude is a joy to be around.

A sense of humor is an invaluable asset to a marriage. In fact, I wonder how a marriage can last for years unless both parties are able to laugh together as they live together. Laughter can bring an end to a dispute, clear the air, and banish the last dregs of anger. You can't stay mad when you are laughing.

In a large family, a sense of humor is a necessity. I suspect it is a necessity in almost every area of our lives. The ability to laugh at ourselves can lighten a tense situation, or keep a person humble. You can't become conceited when you can laugh at your own foibles.

We mountain folk have a unique sense of humor, which is sometimes lost on people from other states. We can laugh at ourselves, laugh with one another, but we resent folks laughing at us—especially outsiders.

An incident that happened several years ago stands out in my mind. A couple of my grandsons had gone to Pocahontas County on a Boy Scout camping trip, and I went with their mother on Parent's Night. They had a speaker from a state up north—possibly New York. This young girl told the assembly how her parents had warned her against barefoot hillbillies making moonshine, pursued by "revenooers." No one laughed, and I don't think anyone even grinned. The joke fell flat on the stage floor, never to rise again.

She grew perturbed and said hastily, "Hey, look—it was just a joke." Still no one laughed, and she finished her talk in a rather flustered manner. I don't remember the gist of her speech, but after such an unfortunate beginning, I don't think it mattered.

This is not a joke book, but an accounting of funny happenings in the life of a country family. Mountain humor may be different from jokes told in more urban areas, but it is unaffected, honest, and quite down to earth.

These stories are all true, and include lots of stories about children—because we have such a flock of them. Some of the stories go back in the years, while others are more current. Human nature being what it is, some things never change.

Those Wonderful Kids

I am thankful that the good Lord gave us a "quiver full" of children—and grandchildren. It would be a dull world without them.

I believe that country kids have more fun than those who grow up in the city. My cousin Kay was a kid raised in the city, but she loved coming to our farm to visit. She would devour corn on the cob (we called them roastin' ears) with gusto, but was especially fond of our macaroni and cheese.

One day Daddy told her to go to the garden and pick some macaroni and Mom would fix it for supper. She spent several minutes wandering around in the garden, and then came back in with a bewildered look. "I couldn't find any!" she said sadly. I'm afraid she endured a lot of teasing from us.

Kids and mud seem to go together; at least, ours did. I'll never forget the Easter Sunday when my sister-in-law Alice and her three little ones stopped in on their way to church to show us their new Easter outfits. The twins, Sheila and Leila, were adorable in their frilly dresses, natural curls and black Mary Jane shoes. Douglas, who was 15 months younger, looked like a little man in a three-piece suit, white shirt, and snappy hat with a feather in the brim.

While they were wandering around in the yard, posing for snapshots and generally being admired, Doug managed to fall in a ditch overflowing with springtime mud. Little ones are a blessing even when you have to scrape the mud off them.

Country kids invent their own fun. We literally lived out children's classics such as *Treasure Island* and *Huckleberry Finn*. We rode down the Mississippi River with Huck and Jim on pieces of corrugated tin nailed together. We floated this on two feet of water in the creek until it sunk and left us sitting on the bottom.

We dug for buried treasure one whole summer, all up and down the creek, leaving holes big enough to fall in and break a leg. We decided that the funny-looking hump in Mom's chicken yard must surely hold the remains of an Indian chief, and we dug a hole big enough to bury a cow. The only treasures we found were a few chicken bones and some broken pieces of Mom's Blue Willow dishes.

Daughter Patty took her boys to Sea World when they were small, and the youngsters were quite impressed. After they returned home, Patty glanced out the window and saw a rope go by very fast, with Luke on the end of it. As she stood there wondering, Aaron flashed by on his bicycle, and she realized that he was towing the rope and Luke. About the third pass around the house, she decided she'd better investigate.

She stepped out on the house and called, "What on earth are you boys doing?" "I'm water skiing, Mom" Luke answered with a wide grin. "Did you see me slide?"

Back in the summer, four-year-old Luke told his Sunday school teacher that "today is my burfday." She gave him a fifty-cent piece. He accepted it and many congratulations from his classmates with a shy grin. After the service, she had a good laugh when she found out his birthday is actually January 2. (He kept the money.)

Last week when his birthday did come due, Patty baked a cake the day before and served cake and ice cream to him and his cousins—it was more convenient for her. The next morning she got him out of bed and said, "Wake up, Lukie, today is your birthday!" He looked at her in astonishment and exclaimed, "Again?"

Abigail informed me the other day that her nose holes are getting bigger. "It's because I pick my nose," she confided. "Oh, you shouldn't do that," I admonished. "I know," she agreed quickly. "I sure don't want it to get like my Daddy's!"

Abigail, who was four at the time, gave me what was probably the supreme compliment of my life. "You know what I'm gonna be when I grow up?" she asked seriously. "A grandmaw!"

⁜

Our grandson Luke has been having sibling rivalry pains toward his baby brother, Adrian. It got worse after Adrian learned to say, "Poppaw's buddy" (this is infringing on Luke's territory.) This morning he pushed Adrian flat on his face. Criss picked him up and lectured Luke, "Shame on you, Lukie, for doing your baby brother like that. He wouldn't do that to you." Luke looked up and said, "Watch him grin!"

After Criss left I tried to smooth things over and told Luke brightly, "Aren't you glad you have a little baby brother?" "Yes," he answered cheerily. "Sometimes he likes for me to kick him!"

⁜

I think Patty's Luke must have inherited some genes from my side of the family. The family was getting ready to take an out of state trip over the Memorial Day holiday when he decided to go horseback riding. He promised to be back soon, but hours passed and Patty grew more and more worried. She had visions of his being thrown from the horse, lying in the woods with a fractured skull or worse.

She called the neighbors and Columbia Gas (he was riding on a pipeline trail) and had the UPS man praying for his safety. After hours of searching, his brother Adrian found him in the top of a tall tree, where he had been stuck for four solid hours.

It seemed that he and a neighbor boy had decided to build a tree house, and the ladder they had used had fallen to the ground and was too heavy for young Chris to lift by himself. Patty stormed at him. "Why in the world didn't you send Chris after someone to help?" "Well, Mom," he answered in sweet reason, "We didn't want anyone to know where our secret tree house was!"

Our children had a favorite grapevine on the hill above the creek, and they would swing out over the creek and back. They had swung on it for a couple of summers, and one spring morning my niece Lisa Ann decided to take a swing before the school bus came. She gave a mighty swing out over the creek; the grapevine broke and dumped her headlong on the rocks and in the water. There went her school clothes.

She thought she was dying, but other than a few scrapes and bruises she was fine. So was Patty when she jumped across the creek (it was wide then, and fairly deep) calling to our pastor, "Lookee here, Junior." She misjudged her distance, and landed right in the middle of a hole of water and disappeared from view.

She always got furious when we laughed at her, and Junior had a hard time keeping a straight face when she reappeared, dripping wet. She wasn't hurt, but was mad as a wet hen.

I loved what three-year-old Scotty said to a family friend. The friend said teasingly, "Scotty, you are as ugly as your Daddy!" Quick as a flash, Scotty retorted, "You are as ugly as my Daddy too!"

John Bill, daughter-in-law Sarah's brother, loved Boy Scouts when he was a kid and was anxious to introduce his grandsons to the club. When Nathaniel was old enough, his grandpa urged him to join. He was less than enthusiastic, and shied away from the idea. He was sort of timid, and simply didn't want to do it.

Then Keaton came along. He was excited about it, and talked constantly about campouts, cooking over a campfire, and all the things that Boy Scouts do. His grandpa noticed that Nathaniel got quiet and thoughtful. Peeping around the bathroom door where John Bill was shaving, he asked in a meek little voice, "Poppa, do Boy Scouts get to come home for Christmas?"

When we first built our house close to my mother and father, I gave the kids strict orders not to eat at their house unless I gave them permission. One day Mike was visiting them at mealtime, and Daddy asked him to eat. "I can't, Poppy—Mommy will whip me if I do." (I wouldn't have.) "Go ahead and eat, Mike," Daddy urged him. "She won't know it." "Yes, she will," Mike answered. "She smells my breath!"

Little Luke, who really is a worker, was helping my mother rake her yard. He told Mom, "I don't work like this for my Mommy. She's mean to me." "She is?" Mom asked in surprise. "I think I'd better come and live with you," Luke continued. "She's been a'wantin' me to leave anyway!" (He was five years old.)

Mandy Boggs rushed home from kindergarten a few days ago and was bubbling over to her mother, "Mommy, my friend Greg has two honky-tonks and he let me play with them all day!" Mystified, Sharon asked, "Honky-tonks? What's that?" Mandy answered impatiently, "Oh, you know, Mommy—you put them up to your ear and talk in them—honky-tonks." Finally Sharon figured out she meant walkie-talkies!

We went mushroom hunting last week with Mike, Peggy and their small daughter Chrissy. We didn't have much luck finding mushrooms, but we covered a lot of territory. Mike took us into such deep woods we thought we might see Indian footprints.

Chrissy was more than a little apprehensive; she kept glancing back over her shoulder as if expecting to see a bear, at the very least. The woods must have looked menacing to a five year old. She held my hand tightly as we made our way through the underbrush, around knotted grapevines, and across fallen logs.

I began noticing large patches of bare earth where leaves and sticks had been scratched away. "Look, Chrissy," I exclaimed. "Wild turkeys must have done this." We came upon more disturbed places, especially around fallen logs. "Chrissy," I said in a loud whisper, "If I scare out a turkey, you grab it." She turned around and looked me straight in the eye and said in no uncertain tone, "YOU grab it—I'm allergic to turkeys!"

When my Aunt May and Uncle Myles were little shavers, they played in the same creek that we frolicked in as kids. It was during one of their swimming escapades that Aunt May attempted suicide. Actually, it was a suicide pact the two had made, but Uncle Myles chickened out at the last minute.

It was hot summertime, and Grandma O'Dell had to go back on the hill to help hoe corn. Grandma left the two young'ins in charge of the house, with strict instructions to stay there and wash the dinner dishes. But the pull of the swimming hole was too strong, so they abandoned their chores and headed for the creek. They were splashing and playing and having a big-eyed time when Grandma returned.

The house had no screen doors, and the chickens had invaded the kitchen and were partaking of the leftovers still on the table. Grandma could hear the children laughing and splashing, so she sneaked up on them with a switch and laid the limb to them.

They sat on the bank nursing their stripes, when they decided to just end it all—and "then she'd be sorry." Uncle Myles talked Aunt May into going first, so she picked up a big rock and chunked herself in the head with it. Immediately a huge purple knot popped out between her eyes. Uncle Myles took one look at it and decided he'd rather live a little longer.

When little Jonathan's mother went on vacation and left him behind, he missed his mother desperately. He made a classic statement; "I'm not homesick, because I'm home. But I sure am Mommy sick!"

My sister Jeannie had a slumber party in a camper with several of her small granddaughters. Katie, age four, told them a fairy tale. She began, "There was this princess, and she was going to Kansas. But she decided to go to the Ball instead." Her older sister, Kelsey, interrupted at this point, "That's not the way it goes, Katie!" Katie was furious. "Shut up, Kelsey—I'm telling this!" she yelled.

She continued, "Her 'very' godmother turned her rags into a dark pink dress, with dark pink shoes. The Prince was at the Ball. Her sisters tore her dress off her, so she decided to go to the Dairy Queen. She had a hamburger and ice cream with sprinkles and caramel sauce. The Prince didn't go to the Dairy Queen. He went to Kansas."

Our family is blessed in having three toddlers who are almost the same age. At almost three, they are learning to play together and share their toys. My niece Kara was watching her daughter Kelsey give some of her toys to another child. "Oh, Kelsey," she praised, "You're sharin'!" Kelsey looked at her mother with enormous dark eyes and replied in a puzzled tone, "No, I'm not—I'm Kelsey!"

Eight-year-old David got in a little fracas with another boy at school, and the boy popped David in the face. When he came home and told his mother Peggy, she said, "Well, you know what the Bible says, David. If someone hits you, you turn the other cheek to him." "I wasn't about to, Mommy," David replied heatedly. "He'd already hit me on one cheek, and I just had one more left!"

Four-year-old Brad's cousin Andrea got a new bicycle this summer, and Brad is green with envy. Andrea was visiting Brad, and rode her bicycle in a small dirt road that ran past their house. Brad's mother stepped out and yelled, "Andrea, get out of that road! A car might come along and run over you!" Quick as a wink Brad asked, "Oh, Mommy, if she gets killed, can I have her bicycle?"

Chris was a tow-headed little boy who spent a lot of time at our house. One day he was swinging on our front porch swing, chewing a wad of green bubble gum so big he could hardly get his teeth down on it. "Where did you get that bubble gum, Chrissy?" I asked. "Oh, I found it beside your walk," he answered. (It was already chewed.) "Chrissy, that's dirty!" I said in horrified tones. "Naw, it's not," he answered calmly; "I washed it with my mouth!"

When Patty visited friends last week, their daughter Debbie took Aaron and three-year-old Luke down to the creek and caught them a bucket of crawdads. Debbie happened to notice that Luke had a stick and was vigorously pounding the contents of the bucket. "Lukie!" she screamed, "Don't! You'll kill the crawdads!" "I not killing them Debbie," he explained sweetly. "I teaching them to fight!"

Two of my sisters-in-law were visiting us, reminiscing about old times. I enjoyed listening to their recollections of the hard times when they were young. They shared many tasks with a neighboring family, such as hoeing corn and putting up hay. One day they were laboring in the hot hay field, and the neighbor's daughter brought them a pail of water to drink.

Tired and thirsty from their backbreaking task, they looked forward to a drink. Just as they got ready to assuage their thirst, the girl piped up, "Don't drink all the water off the bottom—my turtle's in there."

One snowy evening last week, our daughter-in-law Sarah watched for the school bus to stop to let five-year-old Josh off. To her amazement, the school bus sailed right on by without a pause. She called the school to confirm that he had been put on the bus. She dialed my sister who lived a couple of miles on down the road. Mary Ellen ran out and waved both hands at the bus, trying to stop it. Josh looked out the window and smiled sweetly and waved back at her. Almost out to the main road, the bus driver turned around and spied Josh. Josh said calmly, "If you are lookin' for my house, it passed us way back up there!"

A stomach virus has been making its rounds, and three-year-old Chrissie caught the bug. She stumbled in the bathroom, where her father Mike was shaving, looking sick and woebegone. "What's the matter, Sissy?" her daddy asked sympathetically. "Oh Daddy," she wailed, "My belly has the headache!"

When I came home from the hospital after surgery, three-year-old Abigail moped around my bed like a lost soul. Finally I coaxed her up in bed with me, but she was still leery. She lay there a few minutes, and then began coughing. I had a cough drop in my mouth, so I bit it in two and gave her a piece of it. She looked over at me solemnly and said, "Boy, I hope I don't catch your belly!"

Patty said that Luke and Aaron came in the door a day or so ago, and both of them were crying like their hearts were broken. Tears were streaming down three-year-old Lukie's face, so dirty that only the whites of his eyes and two rivulets down his face showed up. Alarmed, she asked, "What on earth is the matter with Lukie?" Six-year-old Aaron explained between sobs, "He's crying because he wants to go to heaven." "Then what is the matter with you?" she asked. Aaron replied, "I'm crying 'cause I don't want him to go!"

Have you ever noticed how much little boys love creeks? David, who is in kindergarten, ventured too near the creek last week and of course he fell in. He was taken home dripping wet and cold and his mother Peggy raked him over the coals. She ended her lecture with, "And I don't even have a dryer to dry your clothes!" David listened in solemn silence, and then said gravely, "I'll tell you one thing, Mommy, when I grow up and have kids they'd better think twice before they do things like this!"

Mike picked Chrissy up from the floor where she was deeply involved in playing with her dolls. He hugged and kissed her as she squirmed to be put back down. "What's the matter, Chrissy, don't you love me?" he asked sort of offended. "Well, yes," she answered impatiently. "But I want to love you from down there!"

Patty told Luke that she believed he was getting fat. "Yes," he answered agreeably. "My belly is growing up!" I think a lot of us have that problem.

As the day draws to a close, the grandchildren are running to and fro on the lawn catching lightning bugs to put in a glass jar. There is never a dull moment around here. Luke just showed up with a brand new haircut that he gave himself—"so Adrian can't pull my hair," he explains. "I can't straighten it up," mourns Pat. It's cut clear into the hide on one side."

Jessica holds her new baby brother Joseph and posses-sively caresses him. "What a sweet little brother," I say as I try to encourage her to share. He's yours and Benji's." Her black eyes snap at me as she retorts, "He's a little bit Benji's, and a whole bunch mine!"

Three-year-old Jessica asked me where I got my purse, and I told her that Patty had bought it for me. She asked, puzzled, "Which Patty?" I explained, "You know—Adrian's mommy." I went on to tell her, "Did you know that your Aunt Patty used to be my little girl, and I was her mommy?" She studied this for a few minutes, and then as understanding dawned on her, exclaimed, "Oh, she growed like a mommy, didn't she?" Faster than you think, I thought to myself.

Sometimes I wonder about my children. Like most mothers, I have to hide the Band-aids because they are used on last year's injuries, freckles and warts. I also hide the Super Glue from Matthew, as he will glue everything that is hanging loose. The other night he found the glue, and took it upstairs with him. We had gone to bed, and in a little while I heard him in the bathroom, making funny noises.

"What's wrong, Matthew?" I asked sleepily. In a muted tone he muttered, "I've got Super Glue up my nose." Wide-awake now, I shouted, "How in the world did you get Super Glue up your nose?" "You think that's bad?" he asked. "A while ago I had my finger glued up in it!" (You can guess how that happened.)

One winter we battled an earache with Andy, when he was four or five years old. I had him to the doctor a couple of times, but still it persisted. Along in the spring I was picking at his ear, and I could see something in it. I got the tweezers and carefully worked the object out. It was a folded-up beech leaf, carefully preserved and almost intact. He had pushed it in there the summer before. Like I say, sometimes I wonder about my kids.

Our world, as observed by our little folk, must be something of a mystery most of the time. On a recent nature walk, four-year-old Luke closely observed the tiny white worms in the hull of a black walnut and asked in wonder, "How do them little worms carry that walnut around?"

Sometimes kids ask questions that are hard to answer, as "How do the leaves change?" Their little minds can't quite grasp the concept of chlorophyll and the effect of low temperatures. It is easier to explain, "God paints the leaves." To tell the truth, I like that explanation better. When the Creator made this beautiful world, He made something that no person can duplicate.

My first cousin Evelyne, who has taught the second grade for many years, collects some gems. Years ago the class decided to write to President Reagan and invite him to their annual Veteran's Day program. "Not that he would come," she explained. "It is just good practice for the children."

Standing before the class, she intoned, "Children, Ronald Reagan is our president." There was a puzzled look from a little boy in the back of the room, then came the astonished query from him, "Well, whatever happened to Abraham Lincoln?" She said she hated to be the one to break the news to him that Abraham Lincoln was dead.

Another time she was teaching the children about the letter "B." "Who can tell me what begins with B?" she asked. A hand shot up in the back of the room and a small boy yelled, "Boltswagon!"

Our six-year-old grandson, David, has formed a singing group with the boys in the first grade. He said all except two boys were included. Mike was all primed to give him a lecture on discrimination, when David explained that he had run out of cards—membership cards, he explained patiently.

Their singing group is called "The Howling Foxes," and they have an original song composed by Brian Legg. David says that Brian is the brains of the group. I didn't catch all the lyrics, but they included, "We like peanut butter, we like cars" and ended with "most of all, we like you!" The ending is sort of a yodel—"youooooooooo!" Brian does the ending because as David says, "He is the best howler we got."

We've had an outbreak of chicken pox recently among the younger generation, and my niece Kara's four-year-old daughter Kelsey was exposed. The night before she broke out with it, Kara tucked her in bed and recited the old childhood saying that we used to repeat to one another, "Good night, sleep tight; don't let the bedbugs bite."

The next morning she woke up liberally covered with little red spots. Kelsey took one look at herself and wailed, "Oh, Mommy, them bedbugs came while I was asleep and chicken-pocked me all over!"

I saw Reuben try to catch a robin a day or so ago. He'd come in the house and asked for "a little bit of salt." It seems that his Poppaw had told him if he would sprinkle some salt on the bird's tail, he would be able to catch it. Armed with his handful of salt, he tried to sneak up on the robin. He would make three stealthy steps, and the bird would take three short hops—the bird seemed to know that he was no real threat.

Little grandson of mine—I hope you will always retain this wide-eyed wonder at the marvels of nature all around us. May you ever thrill at the coming of spring, the glory in a sunset. Most of all, I pray that you will grow up with a deep faith in our great Almighty God who has made all things well.

The smaller grandchildren were exposed to the insect world this summer. Some of their conversations can be quite enlightening, and I have learned a lot from them that I didn't know. A sweat bee stung Rachel, who had just turned five. She was describing it to Reuben, not quite five. "What stung you, Rachel?" he asked curiously. "It was an ant," she replied firmly. "I know, because it had two hind legs and two front legs."

"I know what has two hind legs and no front legs," Reuben announced. "What?" asked Rachel. "A chicken!" he answered triumphantly.

Sometimes Reuben is too smart for his own good. He was staying with Mom one day last week, and scattered his toys all over the living room floor and left them there. Mom told him, "Reuben, you need to pick up your toys," He ignored her, so she decided to try some child psychology. In a confidential tone she said, "You know, Reuben, when Kelsey (another of her great-grandchildren) stays with me, she always picks up her toys.

Reuben pondered over this for a minute, and then said thoughtfully, "Well, maybe she'll come over and pick up mine!"

Little Steven, my sister Jeannie's grandson, is like most boys his age. Like Reuben, he loves to scatter his toys, but hates to pick them up. His mother put him to work recently picking up all his toys that he had spread all over the living room. He obediently complied, but growled, "Don't I ever get a day off around here?"

I love being a mother, and enjoy my children, but there is something special about grandchildren, as most grandparents will tell you. I wonder sometimes if children aren't smarter nowadays when I hear some of the things they say.

I was babysitting three of my grandchildren the other day, Reuben and Rachel, who are both five, and three-year-old Alexandria-called-Judy. It was a warm, sunny day, perfect for children to play outside. I left them playing amiably with a plastic tea set and a great deal of imagination.

In a few minutes, Judy burst through the front door squalling bloody murder. She was drenched with water from head to heels, and spluttered indignantly "Reuben did it." When I collected the "glory details," as a former neighbor used to say, Reuben confessed that he had done the dastardly deed.

He told me, "I poured her some tea (water) in her cup and she wouldn't drink it. So I told her to drink it or wear it." She wore it. He got to sit on a chair until he mulled over his sins and duly repented.

My sister Jeannie's seven-year-old granddaughter Chastity just received her membership into a Brownie troop. She was thrilled to death, and ran in the house shouting, "I get to be a Brownie!" Her cousin, Little Steven, was not to be outdone. "Huh," he bragged, "I'm gonna be a BIG cake!"

Come to think of it, yesterday's kids were pretty swift on the uptake also. When my nephew Noel was just a little fellow, he was suffering from a painful toothache. He moaned and groaned until his mother Susie finally said, "Oh, Noel, don't carry on so—it's not going to kill you! Anyway, you are ready to go, aren't you?" "Yes, I am," he agreed. "But I don't want to die in pain!"

A few weeks ago our son Kevin purchased a new car, and he and Sarah took it out for an initial drive. Of course Reuben, their six-year-old, wanted to go along. Sarah explained to him, "Now this car is equipped with airbags, and you will have to sit in the back seat because they have been known to inflate and injure children.

He dutifully hopped into the back seat. And when they returned, their daughter Abigail, who is 16, was waiting in the driveway for her turn. Reuben jumped out of the car and advised her, "Now Sissy, you will probably want to sit in the back seat—there's a couple of windbags up front!"

Reuben stayed with us when his mother went to France with a group of students from high school. She called on Sunday, and asked to speak to Reuben. I passed the phone to him, and he listened for a minute, looked up at me, and said in an astonished tone, "She's speaking English!"

Sometimes growing up is hard, and the first marriage

in a family is traumatic. Reuben came over to our house the night before his older brother Joshua was getting married. With a woebegone face he told us, "I'm sleeping with Josh tonight—it's his last night at home."

It reminded me of their father Kevin's wedding. We had four sons at home and two sets of bunk beds in one room. Our youngest son, Matthew, would not sleep in his bunk, but would crawl in bed with Kevin every night. (Kevin was six feet and four inches tall, and Matthew was ten years old and they were sleeping in one tiny bunk.) That was carrying family togetherness to the limit.

The first night alone, Matthew was lying in his bunk sobbing softly. From the adjoining bedroom, his little sister Crystal called, "Do you want to sleep with me, Bubby?" He answered sadly, "No, Sissy, I'll just have to get used to it!" I guess we all have to get used to it.

Sex education is a subject that comes naturally enough here in the hills among the farm animals and wildlife. Perhaps we take it too much for granted that children assimilate the knowledge on their own. When Jeremy was about twelve, Patty called me much amused. "Mommy," she informed me, "Someone is going to have to tell Jeremy the facts of life."

He had gotten into a discussion with her three boys about the birds and bees, and the results were hilarious. It had started with the subject of puberty. One of the boys had asked Patty how they would know when they reached that stage.

Patty began to explain to them, "Well, there are signs

you will notice—your voice will begin to change, and you will grow hair on your chest."

Here she was interrupted by Jeremy, who muttered, ""Ugh, gross, I don't want hair on my chest!"

Patty continued, "Jeremy, you will probably have a lot of hair on your chest, as boys generally take after their fathers, and Mike has a lot."

He brightened. "I know a boy who will never have hair on his chest," he announced. "He doesn't have a father."

Patty said patiently, "Jeremy, everyone has a father!"

Jeremy was adamant. "This boy doesn't have one."

Patty persisted, "Jeremy, it takes a mother and father both to have a baby."

By now Jeremy was getting indignant. "I saw on television (the final authority I guess) that 45 percent of American men are having their own babies!"

"What on earth has he been watching?" Patty asked me.

Patty tried to explain to him, but he stuck to his guns. "I hope my daddy has a baby," he expostulated in loud tones. "Then you will see that I am right!" (And wouldn't Mike be surprised!)

At least he didn't go out in the woods and try to find babies in the dry leaves like Mary Ellen and I used to do. Somewhere we had gotten the idea that babies were found there, and we wanted so much to find one.

I think it was because of a brood sow we had at one time. One day she was just a big, fat hog, and the next day there were 13 little piglets rooting for their dinner. "Where did they come from, Mommy?" we asked with interest.

"Oh, she probably dug them up in the woods," she answered airily.

Although we scratched around in the woods all summer, we never did find a baby.

Morgan and Molly are sisters, with less than a year between them. At four, Morgan is pretty bossy with Molly, and sometimes screams at her when she is displeased. Their grandmother Sarah was babysitting them, and she heard Morgan loudly railing at Molly. "All right, young lady, that is enough," Sarah ordered. "You just stop that right now—just chill out!"

Morgan disappeared, and Sarah found her in her bedroom with the door closed. As soon as she saw her grandmother, she said with great dignity, "Now get out and shut the door, Nana—I'm chilling up!"

Molly is a candy addict. When she was just a little tot, she would make her rounds at church bumming candy. Of course Regina didn't allow her to do that, but she became adept at panhandling. She was allowed to rummage in her grandmother and great-grandmother's purses, and would look longingly at the other ladies' pocketbooks.

She reminded us of Jeannie's Steven. He could be sitting in the back of the church, and if someone rattled a candy paper on the front pew, Steven would appear as if by magic. Molly was just like him—she had a nose for candy.

One Sunday morning she must have made a dry run. She climbed up on Criss' lap and said in disgust, "Some of these people don't bring anything but theirselves to church!"

The other night after church, she wandered in Mom-Granny's (her great-great grandmother) bedroom and came out eating a stick of candy. I asked her, "Don't you think you ought to give Mom-Granny a piece of that? After all, it is her candy." She looked at Mom and grinned, then said, "Naw—she might get her dress dirty!"

Molly and Morgan's brother, three-year-old Hunter, has entertained us all evening. I believe that child was born talking. My sister Mary Ellen was here and I told her that he has always talked like an adult. I noticed his face was downcast, and I asked him what was wrong. He replied quickly, "You said I was a dolt, and I'm not a dolt!"

Morgan and Molly Ann were eating dinner at Papa-Kevin's the other day, and two-year-old Molly asked for some more "p'sagna." Morgan, like the usual older sister, immediately corrected her. "It's 'per-sagna'" she said firmly. That's better than "la-sag-ney" as baby sister Susie called it.

My brother Larry's granddaughter, Bonnie Lynn, once told me of a "tack" cat she owned. "A 'tack' cat?" I asked curiously. "Yes," she went on to explain. "When you walk through the house, it 'tacks' you!"

I'll never forget my nephew, Brian, when he was just a little fellow, asking me for a "cat." He didn't speak too plainly at that age, and I kept questioning him as to the kind of cat he wanted. Finally he exclaimed in exasperation, "Just a cat—you know, like Bugs Bunny!" (He wanted a carrot.)

When great-granddaughter Bekah (Rebekah) started talking, she spoke with a definite lisp. When her sister Savannah came along, we heard her giving her younger sister speech lessons. "Say 'wug' (rug)" she instructed. Savannah obediently repeated, "Wug!" Further lessons were canceled.

Granddaughter Taylor, almost three years old, was here for the day last week. (I think she's been here ever since.) She chattered incessantly as she "helped" me in the kitchen, with every sentence beginning, "My mommy said . . ." She had eaten three Popsicles, and asked for a fourth. I told her I didn't think she needed another Popsicle, and she answered firmly, "My mommy said that I needed a perfect Popsicle." She got it.

Life on the farm can be humorous. Our youngest grandson, Nicholas, who will be three next month, came through the yard carrying something for his Poppaw. He proudly presented a baby blacksnake, alive and wiggling, to his startled grandfather. Criss has a paranoid fear of snakes, even baby ones. He dispatched this one in a hurry.

"But he's a good snake," Nicholas protested. Criss didn't think it was funny, but I did.

※⇒◎⇐※

Mild September days drift down, like early falling leaves on the hilltops and the ridges and hollers. The hurried pace of summer slows down as the late garden crops are harvested and put away.

There is more time now to roam the woods and gather some of the wild foods that nature has to offer. I've asked the grandsons to be on the lookout for elderberries as they rummage through the woods. Josh is digging ginseng and yellow root, and 11-year-old Adrian is following in my footsteps. Almost every day he takes a bag to the woods to look for herbs.

He is a frustrated woodsman. Yesterday, I found the remains of a cabin he had constructed, and earlier this summer he piled pine boughs and moss on a wooden frame extended over the creek. "It's a lean over," he explained, "so I won't get hot fishing!"

※⇒◎⇐※

Grandchildren and grandparents are made for each other. We have time to slow our steps to match those of a small grandchild, patience to wait while the little one examines the wonder of a busy anthill, or take a walk to the garden and look for the last few ripe raspberries. Small grandchildren think that their grandparents are perfect, and we know the grandchildren are.

※⇒◎⇐※

I can always count on Reuben to help with any project. I went to the garden to set out some Dutch onions, when Reuben appeared from nowhere. "I want to help you, Mommaw," he said. I gave him the bag of onion sets, and proceeded to dig holes for them, as the ground was pretty hard. He was content for a while dropping the sets into the holes I dug, after admonishing me sternly, "Don't hit me in the head with the hoe like you did yesterday!"

Soon he was begging to dig the holes. "You can't do it, Reuben," I told him. "The ground is too hard, and you are too little." "I can so, too" he retorted. "I can huff and puff just like you!" So we huffed and puffed together and planted the onions.

Mom enjoys her great grandchildren as much as she did her grandchildren. Two of them, Rachel, age four, and Judy, live near her. They visit her frequently and "help" with whatever task she is doing outside.

The other day, they were joined by my sister Jeannie's granddaughter, Kelsey, who is almost four. Mom was raking leaves, and they helped her finish the task.

They left for home, and Mom was watching them walk out to the driveway when Kelsey suddenly wheeled around and came back to the house. As Mom opened the door for her, she looked at Mom with liquid brown eyes and announced, "I've come back to keep an eye on you!" (Mom is almost 80.)

She seated herself on the couch, crossed her legs, and continued, "And I think I'll just have a little snack while I'm at it!" She got her snack.

Kara was babysitting a little girl who came one morning with her fingernails painted bright red. Kelsey was consumed with envy. "Mommy, I want you to paint my fingernails red," she requested. Kara patiently explained to her that she was to leave her fingernails just like the Lord made them.

That night when she went in the bedroom to listen to her prayers and tuck her in bed, she found Kelsey staring at the ceiling. "Mommy," she said thoughtfully, "I think I'll just ask the Lord to give me some of them red fingernails!"

My nephew Eric took his five-year-old daughter Madison with him when he ran an errand. On the way home, he stopped and bought her a bag of candy, which she began to devour with gusto. "Maddie," Eric asked, "Don't you think you should save your sisters some of that candy?" "Naw," Maddie answered. "They already know what it tastes like!"

⊹⇒◉⇐⊹

We have tried to instill in our children the need to thank God for our blessings. At an early age, they learned to thank the Lord before a meal for the food set before them.

When my sister Mary Ellen's son Danny was a little boy, they returned from the grocery store laden with bags of groceries. Danny looked at the mountain of groceries piled on the kitchen counter and asked in all seriousness,

"Daddy, why don't you ask the blessing over all this food and then you won't have to say it every time we eat!"

⋆⇒◉⇐⋆

Believe it or not, Danny (now called Stuart) had a finicky appetite when he was small. You know the routine. "Take a bite for Mommy, now take a bite for Daddy, now take a bite for the puppy!"

They were eating dinner with his Grandmother Friend one day when Danny turned up his nose at a full plate of food and declared, "I'm too full to eat another bite!" Mrs. Friend said wisely, "Well, I guess he's too full to eat any ice cream then." Danny replied quickly, "Oh, I saved a hole for that!"

He once prayed a unique prayer. He'd been quite difficult one evening, fighting with his brothers and being generally obnoxious. Finally Mary Ellen lost patience with him. "Take him upstairs. Howard, and put him to bed," she told his father.

When they got upstairs, he refused to say his prayers. His father insisted, so he got down on his knees and prayed the usual "Now I lay me down to sleep." Then he added, "God bless Mommy and Daddy and Freddie and David, and I hope the devil gets every one of them!"

⋆⇒◉⇐⋆

My sister-in-law once lived in a neighborhood with a young man, who wasn't too smart. He was visiting her one day and confided that his sister was expecting a baby. She responded politely, "How nice!" "Yeah," he went on, "I do hope it is a boy or a girl one!"

One of my little boys was watching me bathe the current newborn (years ago) and asked with absorbed interest, "What is it going to be when it grows up, Mommy—a boy or a girl?"

Matthew was born when our oldest son Michael was 12. Michael had a nonchalant attitude about him, and I asked Mike what he thought of his baby brother. He replied, "Well, he ain't no Rock Hudson!"

When our children were growing up, they made do with whatever they could find to play with. We didn't have a yard full of motorcycles, four-wheelers, and battery-powered toys. I remember the time Mike and Kevin acquired an old motorcycle when they were just gangly boys. Unfortunately, it was motor-less. They would push the contraption to the top of an oil well road, then take turns coasting it to the bottom of the hill—with visions of Evel Knievel dancing through their heads.

It was Mike's turn to ride the vehicle. Kevin was stationed at the foot of the hill, where a heavy gate was opened wide. His job was to watch for cars on the main road and warn the brakeless rider.

Kevin always had the mildest temperament of all our children, but a devil must have gotten in him that day. Just as Mike reached the gate, Kevin closed it. I didn't hear the crash, but sounds of shouting and mayhem drew me to the porch.

Kevin's behind was closer to the ground then than it is

now, and Mike had him by the arm kicking it all the way to the house. For days, it was dangerous to mention that motorcycle in Mike's hearing.

The Irish have always been known for their love of storytelling, and tales of elves, fairies and leprechauns delight the children. Our granddaughter Brionna, who is six years old, came out of her Sunday school class all excited. She grabbed her mother's arm and said loudly, "Mommy, guess what we learned in Sunday school today?"

Crystal shushed her a little, and then asked, "What did you learn?" Her dark eyes snapping, Brionna answered, "We learned about the ten leprechauns that Jesus healed, and only one came back to give Him thanks!"

Crystal was teaching her girls some stories out of the Old Testament, including Moses and the Ten Commandments. When she got to the part about the children of Israel worshipping the golden calf, Alyssa began crying, "I don't want to do it!" "You don't want to do what?" questioned their mother. "I don't want to warsh-up a golden calf!" she wailed. Indignantly she said, "I don't want to warsh a cow, not with soap, not with water, not with anything!"

The girls went with their father Jeff to the Volunteer Fireman's annual Christmas party, and came home to tell their mother about it. "Did you have a good time?" Crystal asked Brionna. "Oh, yes," she answered with enthusiasm. "One of the fireman read about Jesus being born, and about Murry and Joseph." Then she stopped in bewilderment and said, "I thought murry was what the wise men brought Jesus!" (Oh, that southern accent!)

Life in the country may be quiet, but it is seldom boring. With three great-grandchildren living across the driveway, and two grandchildren on the other side of the garden, we are never lonely. Although they all have chores to do, they find plenty of time to play. There are lightning bugs to catch at dusk, snails and lizards to capture, and plenty of earthworms to collect.

Katie, one of the great-grandchildren from Looneyville, especially likes to catch animal life. She has petted a box turtle, a snail, and numerous worms this summer. We heard her the other day crooning a lullaby, and found her on the porch swing putting an earthworm to sleep.

Kids are funny, and certainly add spice to our lives. Crystal's youngest daughter, Mylie, was helping her do laundry recently. She brought Crystal a load of dirty clothes, including her daddy's briefs. "Mommy," she said in horror, "I've touched my daddy's underwear—now I'll have to live with it the rest of my life!"

Our granddaughter Taylor was in the kitchen watching me prepare supper when she said, "Mommaw, you've got a cider gnat!" "Where?" I asked. She answered quickly, "Right above that apple you are going to peel for me!" She got her apple.

In Sunday school class last Sunday, the teacher asked the preschoolers, "Can anyone tell me what Adam was made of?" Before anyone else could answer, Nicholas shouted, "Blood and guts!"

In another class, the teacher asked, "What was rained down on Sodom and Gomorrah?" Quick as a wink little Roger replied, "Fire and Flintstone!"

Our son Matthew was telling his four-year-old son Jake about spring, and how the birds were singing, and the grass was turning green. Jake listened and then said solemnly, "Daddy, I know what is down under the grass—grasserhops!"

The gardens may be threatened by wild animals, stunted from the drought and heat, but the grandchildren are growing like weeds in a wet spell. Granddaughter Taylor, who weighs almost 20 pounds at five months, is a chubby, lovable, armload of joy. It is hard to keep from spoiling her—and we don't try very hard.

Her older brother, Nicholas, who will turn four this month, has had his share of sibling rivalry. He looks upon his Aunt Patty as his own personal property, and hates for her to hold his sister. Patty was holding her the other day when Nicholas jammed his cowboy hat down upon the baby's head, and tightened the strings under her chin (chins) until her eyes bugged out.

Patty yelled, "Don't, Nicholas, you are choking her." Nicholas never turned a hair, but said calmly, "She likes it tight!"

My four-year-old great-granddaugher got a little taste of punishment a while back when she dropped her kitten off the bridge to the creek below, and her mother saw her. When questioned, she lied and said her two-year-old sister Savannah had done the foul deed.

Her mother Krystal explained to her, "Bekah, I am going to have to spank you for three things. First, you got on the bridge, which is not allowed, and Savannah followed you. She could have gotten on the road and got hit by a car. Second, you dropped the kitten in the creek. Third, you lied about it."

She turned Bekah across her lap and applied the necessary punishment. Bekah wailed, "I can't believe this is happening!"

In this changing world, some things never change. Bible principles never change, children never change, and the need for correction never changes.

Our grandson Nicholas, age six, got on the school bus one morning still half asleep. I should add here that Nicholas marches to a different beat. Super intelligent, he lives in his own world.

The school bus makes a run to Valley Fork Elementary School, where Nicholas is a first grade student, then transports the rest of the children on to Clay. Nicholas was fast asleep when the students got off the bus at Valley Fork. And when the bus driver got to Clay he found this little boy who didn't belong there.

Instead of being scared, Nicholas was thrilled at the adventure. Someone called Transportation, and Mr. Jerry Linkinoggor, County Superintendent of Clay County Schools, volunteered to take him back to Valley Fork.

The roads were snow-covered and icy, and he rode along in style in Mr. Linkinoggor's four-wheel drive vehicle. They made small talk, and Nicholas commented, "These roads are really bad—somebody should have called school off!"

Mr. Linkinoggor hid a smile and asked, "Nicholas, do you know who calls school off?" Nicholas answered quickly, "Why Mr. Schoonover does—he's the boss of the world!" (Mr. Schoonover is the principal at Valley Fork Elementary.)

Nicholas was born talking, and he never met a stranger. He started talking plainly before he was a year old. It was a common sight to see him walk up to someone he had never met, stick out his hand, and announce, "My name is Nicholas. What's your name?"

He was three when his little sister Taylor was born, and although he loved her, he was less than enthusiastic about the attention she received. When he visited his mom in the hospital, he begged her to come home. When she told him she had to stay, he climbed in bed beside her and stated, "I have a fever."

Just then the nurse came in and he told her, "I need an IV!"

Nicholas's mother and grandmother Barbara took him to "Jumpin' Gut" where Barb was raised. There is a place in Clay County called "Jumpin' Gut," as well as "Twist and Shoot" and "End of the World Rocks." His grandmother wanted to go back and visit the old home place.

On the way back, they decided to take a short cut on a path through the woods. Nicholas looked around in deep dismay at the deep woods surrounding them, and then cried dramatically, "We're lost! We're doomed!"

At Christmastime Jennifer and Andy took Nicholas to the mall to visit good Saint Nick, and I think it was an experience for the old man himself. This little three-year-old climbed up on Santa's knee, looked him in the eye, and demanded, "What are you doing here? You are supposed to be at the North Pole, making things!"

Nicholas is so dramatic. He overheard the boys talking about killing a spike buck, and he ran through the house crying, "They've killed my friend! They've killed my friend Spike!" Maybe he thought it was one of Santa's apprentice reindeer.

Jennifer and Andy made a trip to Twin Falls that same summer and it was a long ride home. Nicholas was strapped in his car seat, and he got tired and bored. He generally takes good care of his toys, but this day, out of boredom, he tore up one of his good storybooks.

Jennifer was fit to be tied, and began lecturing him severely. "You know better than to destroy your books," she scolded him. "I'm sorry, Mom," he replied. She kept on, "I'll have to punish you for this!" "Sorry, Mom," he repeated. Jennifer continued, "You can't have toys or privileges for a week!" For the third time, he told her he was sorry. In the pause that followed, he looked up and said sadly, "'Sorry' just doesn't cut it, does it Mom?"

That reminded me of our son Kevin when he was about the same age. He was begging his father for some privilege that his dad had denied. He began crying, and said through his tears, "My tears don't mean a thing to you anymore, do they, Dad?"

Alyssa, our daughter Crystal's four-year-old, was asked to say grace while she and her cousin Megan shared a bowl of chicken noodle soup. She bowed her head and prayed seriously, "Lord, we thank you for this food. We thank you for this day. Help me and Megan and Rachel and Judy and Nicholas and Brionna not to get sick. And Lord, Santa Claus is the best grandpa in the whole world!"

I'm afraid I sort of lost it at that point, and I'm not sure how she finished her grace. She hates to be laughed at, so I took a coughing spell. She probably prayed for my cough. She does have complete faith in her prayers.

Her nose is slightly out of joint since her baby sister, Brionna, came along in May to share the limelight. She is sensitive to the least slight, and we have to be careful not to pay too much attention to the baby—or even a cousin. She and Megan had played amiably all afternoon, until Megan wanted to play with a doll that had belonged to Alyssa's mother, Crystal, when she was a baby.

Alyssa refused to let her have it, but soon laid it down on the bed and forgot it. Megan seized the opportunity, and snatched it up, her dark eyes sparkling with mischief. I got tickled and said, "Megan, I love you!" Then I noticed Alyssa standing there, looking downcast. Hastily, I told her, "Alyssa, I love you too." She folded her arms across her chest, stomped her foot, and asserted, "I hate everybody!"

"Oh, Alyssa," I told her, "Jesus doesn't want you to hate anyone. He wants you to love everybody." Undaunted, she demanded, "Well, what does God say?" (I guess she wanted a second opinion.)

Our baby chickens are hatching, and they are miniature puffs of down. They are irresistible, and Nicholas begged fervently for just one baby chicken. I reasoned with him that one baby chicken by itself would be very lonely, and besides, he didn't have anywhere to put it.

He made three trips down in one day to see the chickens. After he left the last time, I found a pair of his socks beside the box the chickens were in. The next visit, I asked him if he had left a pair of socks here. "Yes," he admitted sheepishly. "I was going to put chickens in them!"

It doesn't matter how many new babies are born into our large and growing family, each one is greeted with the same love and enthusiasm as the first one. Crystal had her newborn daughter, Mylie, here a couple of weeks ago, and the young cousins all crowded around her, counting toes and fingers.

Seven-year-old Nicholas suddenly exclaimed, "Look! She's lost her extension cord!"

※

My sister Jeannie had family in for Thanksgiving. Her niece Kim admonished her five-year-old daughter, Danielle, "Now eat all of your food and you can have a reward. Do you know what a reward is?" "Sure," Danielle answered airily, "It's one of those bumps that gets on your skin!"

That reminded me of when our grandson Adrian shot a mole with his BB gun. "Hey, Grandma—I shot a wart!" he yelled.

※

Jeannie's grandson Seth, who was four years old at the time, came running in from play crying, "Whobody hit me in the head!" If you didn't know who did it, "whobody" would be a lot more descriptive than "somebody."

※

Granddaughter-in-law Regina brought Morgan and Molly over to visit Mom the other day. They are less than a year apart, but quite different in temperament. Morgan is quiet and ladylike, but Molly is a live wire.

Molly wandered around the living room for a while, and then sat down on the couch beside me. After about 45 minutes, their mother told them "Well, girls, we better be going. I have more laundry to do." Molly looked up at me seriously and remarked, "I figured you were going to ask us if we wanted a snack or something!"

Our son-in-law Jeff got so hungry for fresh corn that he picked an armload of blisters and cooked them. Crystal was busy with the baby, but she said the little girls, Alyssa and Brionna, plus their father, were busy buttering and eating them with great gusto. Jeff urged Crystal to hurry up and get in on the repast. She buttered an ear, ate a few bits, then told Jeff, "This is awful—it tastes just like the cob!" Jeff replied cheerfully, "Yes, but ain't it good for cobs?"

One of her uncles was teasing five-year-old Samantha about her baby brother and asked her, "How in the world could you love such an ugly baby?" Samantha thought for a moment, then replied solemnly, "Well, she's part of the family!"

Our grandson Josh grabbed Molly Ann, age four, in a tight hug just after she'd had a bath. Burying his nose in her soft neck, he exclaimed, "Oooh, Molly, you smell good. What have you got on?" She looked at him and said innocently, "Just my dress and panties!" These are moments that are priceless.

Ominous black clouds moved closer in the evening sky, coming faster as the wind increased. Our granddaughter-in-law Regina and her little ones hurried in the house as the storm drew nearer. She had brought the girls and her four-week-old baby to visit, and Mom was anxiously waiting for the baby.

Morgan and Molly crowded around Mom as she cradled baby Hunter in her arms, and just then the storm struck. Loud cracking sounds came from the porch and skylight. Someone asked, "What was that? It sounds like hail!" Just then, hailstones began hitting the skylight so hard that we hurriedly moved Mom and the baby to the couch, as her recliner was positioned right under the skylight.

It seemed any minute that the glass was going to break and crash down upon us. The hailstorm raged on, with stones as big as golf balls, and soon had covered the lawn like a snowstorm. We were so excited about the hail that we didn't notice the deluge of water that poured off the hill and ran across the lawn like a wide river.

The girls were excited, but scared too, as they huddled close to Mom. I came in the bedroom to unplug the computer, with Morgan at my heels. She said softly, "I'm just trying to keep all of you safe!" I realized then that she was trying to keep all of us in one place.

⊹⇒◉⇐⊹

Sibling rivalry exists in almost every family, and I have to be careful not to favor any of the grandkids. This lesson was brought home to me again the other night at church. Judy had won a trophy for reading in her kindergarten class, and had it hidden under her coat. She proudly showed it to me. I told her how proud I was of her, and gave her a dollar bill. I didn't know that her four-year-old sister Megan was watching. As soon as Judy left, she sat down beside me. I hugged her and told her I loved her.

She looked up at me with her huge brown eyes and said, "I'm not very big!" "Yes, you're just little," I replied. Rachel (her older sister) beats on me all the time." (I am so dense that I still didn't catch it.) "Oh, I am sorry," I sympathized with her. Then with a woebegone look, she added, "Rachel won't even let me touch her!" "Oh, dear," I answered. Then all in a rush she said, "I need a dollar!"

Patty was in the mall recently with her two little granddaughters, Rebekah (Bekah) age four, and Savannah, who is going on two. They made a visit to the pet store and the girls were enchanted. "Wook, Nana," said Bekah. "There's a parent bird!" Mystified, Patty asked, "What's a parent bird?" "You know," Bekah replied, "Polly want a cwacker! Polly want a cwacker!"

Sometimes I feel like a parent bird—or maybe a grandparent bird. The nest is full to overflowing many times. When my own children were growing up, we always had a house full of youngsters. Bert Drake, who worked for Clay Lumber Company at the time, asked me just how many children Criss and I had.

I replied that we had six, wondering why he asked. "Well, he continued, "I passed your house the other day and there were 17 in the yard!" That was about right.

Psalm 127:3 says, "Lo, children are a heritage of the

Lord; and the fruit of the womb is his reward." The Lord has provided us with a good heritage.

Six-year-old Katie is in Girl Scouts this year. At a meeting the other day, the girls entered a poster contest with the theme of saving the environment. Katie carefully drew an elegant unicorn with an American flag in its teeth, and titled "Save the Unicorn."

Romance

It's graduation time again, and the viney honeysuckle is spread all over the banks of the old high school. Its heart-wrenching fragrance will always and forever bring back in vivid detail memories of my own high school graduation.

That milestone must surely be one of the most emotional events in the life of an adolescent. In a small high school, four years of togetherness forges ties that are not easily broken. It all seems to culminate on graduation night into a tense knot in the stomach, a heart near to breaking, and tears too close to the surface.

I remember the tears spilled over after I accepted my diploma and walked down the aisle toward freedom and approaching adulthood. At 16, I was not ready. My escort that night was the boy that I had a terrible crush on all through high school.

He was tall and handsome—a star basketball player. I was a mousy bookworm who stood in the shadows and worshipped him from afar. Our senior year, we had some classes together, and he began to notice me—or perhaps he felt the admiring glances that I sent his way. At any rate, he began to walk me to class, and (be still, my heart!) hold my hand.

Graduation night came too soon. I can't remember if he

asked me to walk with him, or I asked him. I do remember how he steadied me when my eyes flooded with tears as we left the old high school forever. He asked me out that night, and then our ways parted.

That was May, 1952. After 46 years, one husband, six children, 17.8 grandchildren and one great-grandchild later, our paths again crossed. One bright sunny afternoon, my husband Criss, brother Ronnie and I were lounging in the living room when Criss remarked, "There's a strange car pulling up in our driveway." An unfamiliar lady pecked on the open door. And I stepped out on the porch to talk to her. She smiled and said, "I've brought someone to see you, and I want you to guess who it is!"

It was then I saw the still tall, still handsome man step out of the car. I had a sinking premonition who it was, and it was. His first words were, "Remember who you marched with at our high school graduation?"

There I stood. I had on an old skirt (we were dressed to go work in the garden) with violent pink and chartreuse ferns printed on the fabric. At least my pink knit shirt matched, but it was too short in the tail and decorated with a smear of orange spaghetti sauce that I'd had for lunch. I had on purple—yes, purple!—canvas shoes, and my hairdo had collapsed over the weekend like a tent in a windstorm. My allergies were acting up, and my nose was drippy.

I invited them in the house where the aroma from the kitchen made it obvious that we were having a pot of brown beans for supper. The sweeper stood in the middle of the floor, waiting for a burst of housewifely energy. Was I surprised? I think overwhelmed is the word.

He was great, though—tanned, self-assured, and with all of his hair—not even very gray. I felt like the tongue-tied, awkward kid that I was in high school. The cool morning had turned quite warm, but I hadn't turned on the air conditioner. I sat on the couch opposite him, and could feel my face steadily growing hotter and hotter. (It wasn't true, as Criss later told, that I sunk deeper and deeper into the couch until only the tips of my purple shoes showed.)

Criss knew of my adolescent crush, and he was thoroughly enjoying the situation. I shot him a look that could kill and said in syrupy tones, "Honey, would you please turn on the air conditioner? It is getting warm in here." Warm? My face looked and felt like a boiled beet. I wasn't about to get up and cross the room, since the 20 pounds I had gained since high school had nowhere to hide.

We did have a pleasant visit, and his sister (it wasn't his wife after all) and I had mutual acquaintances. I was really glad to see him and flattered that he had looked me up to say, "Hello." (Or was it "help" that I heard him say?") But why couldn't it have been on a day when I had at least combed my hair, or didn't have on my oldest clothes to wear to the garden?

After they left, Criss leered at me as maliciously as he could with a black eye patch on one eye. (He had suffered a recent eye injury.) He slapped on his straw hat to go to the garden and I said, "Okay, Panama Jack, when your old flame crosses your path and you've just come in from scattering manure on the north 40, or just crawled out from under the ton truck all covered with oil, it would be poetic justice.

Courting in the hills was a different proposition from today. Youngsters now are so sophisticated compared to the children we were. I see little girls dressed in high-heeled shoes, floating in "Musk" perfume and possessing an air of experience we didn't own at eighteen. As grade school girls, the only cologne we were acquainted with was "Blue Waltz." It was a sure Christmas gift if a boy drew your name at school.

The only scents I remember Mom wearing were "Emeraude" and "Orange Blossom." When we got to be teenagers, the staple was "Evening in Paris" with the blue bottle and silver top. How glamorous we felt in our broomstick skirts that hit the tops of our bobby socks and saddle oxfords! It is amazing to me how we ever got a boyfriend.

The course of true love does not always run smooth, and little things have spoiled many a romance. It makes a person wonder what course their life would have taken if circumstances had been different. Things that were so terribly embarrassing to us as teenagers wouldn't matter a whit now.

Mom was once turned off by a boyfriend because he had missed a little patch of whiskers when he shaved—and there went a budding romance. I liked a boy in high school and after we graduated, he asked to take me to a movie. He bought me a bag of popcorn, and I promptly got choked on the first bite and coughed through the whole show. I was so embarrassed that I couldn't look him in the eye after that. Another romance spoiled.

My granddaughter Jessica is a lot like me. A boy took her for a quick lunch at a fast food place, and her chicken sandwich fell apart in her lap. She was humiliated, and that was the end of that.

Some things are worse. My niece Alison went snowboarding on her first date with Sid. She got sick and barfed down her ski suit. It must have been true love—he married her anyway, and now they have a beautiful baby girl who barfs on both of them.

My sister Jeannie had a date with her boyfriend Jim for the prom. Jim's friend Tommy drove them in his old car, which had the floorboards out of it. Jeannie was dressed fit to kill in her prom gown and was floating in French perfume. Jim had on a white dinner jacket and was also groomed to the teeth.

The car was burning drip gas and on the way developed engine trouble. The fumes were competing with Jeannie's perfume, and Jim ended up under the hood working on the motor. It must not have discouraged them—they recently celebrated their 45th wedding anniversary.

I wonder if this runs in the family. Their son Steven went to pick up his date for their high school prom, dressed up in a tux and carrying a bouquet of flowers. Just as he knocked on the front door, the porch collapsed with him. Her father opened the door to see Steve standing below him, still clutching the flowers.

His brother Eric was dancing with a beautiful girl at the prom (not the same one) while chewing a stick of gum. (I don't know where he got the idea he could dance and chew gum at the same time,) He accidentally dropped his wad of chewing gum in the top of the girl's hairdo. He serenely danced on, with his chin on the top of her head, and chewed furiously. He managed to retrieve the whole wad, hair and all.

I won't even go into sister Susie's escapades—how she hid in the chicken house to hide from an unwanted suitor, and once crawled under a bed. I am surprised that she ever got married at all.

Whether the course is smooth or rough, love is here to stay. But sometimes you wonder about the road not taken . . .

It seemed that we enjoyed our childhood much longer than kids do today, who rush as fast as they can into the realm of adults. Back in the long-ago days of childhood, Mary Ellen and I would build our summer playhouse in the empty corncrib. On rainy days, we would retreat to our own private world and shut the door.

There we bedded down our dolls, (and sometimes ourselves) and listened to the rain beat a tattoo on the tin roof. How safe and contented and cozy we felt! Sometimes we played in the barn on rainy days, and I can still remember that dry dusty hay smell, and the warm, homey odor of the cows. The barn also had a tin roof, and we would burrow back in the hayloft while the rain made music overhead. Today's children are missing so much. They start thinking about girlfriends and boyfriends in the first grade. If they only knew—childhood is so fleeting, and you are hopefully married a long, long time.

Family Blunders and Jokes

Early one morning Mom sent Mark and Ronnie, my youngest brothers, to hoe out the garden. They were grown boys, young men really, and they had an old car minus a motor that they pushed around. They shoved their vehicle to the upper end of the garden and supposedly began their gardening chores.

Along about ten o'clock Mom looked out, and seeing absolutely no movement, she decided to investigate. She quietly slipped up to the old car, and sure enough, both boys and Freckles the dog were curled inside fast asleep. Still silently, she opened the car door just wide enough to get her arm inside; then she poured birch tea on both boys and the dog. Soon they finished their job.

My siblings and I prevailed on Mom to buy a microwave oven. She lives by herself and one would be handy to prepare food and to warm the food we take her. She resisted the idea and refused to consider one. We got together and bought her one, as we figured she'd like it once she got used to it.

She bought some of those "lunch buckets" and put one in her oven. The instructions said to turn it on for one and one quarter minutes. She misread the label and microwaved the contents for 14 minutes. She spent the rest of the morning cleaning up the microwave oven. She eventually conquered the machine—at least she learned how to warm her food.

⊰⟞⊜⊜⟝⊱

We live in an exciting place. One typical evening last week, Patty and I were watching my niece Julie and grandson Jeremy go through a cheerleading routine on the bridge over the creek. Just then Jeremy stepped up on the rail of the bridge, and I gasped, "Oh, that's where his daddy fell and cut his head open when he was little!" Patty said, "Jeremy just fell off, Mom."

We pulled him out of the creek, soaked and bleeding. It looked as if his head was cut open from forehead to chin, and he was shaking uncontrollably from the cold water and shock. When we finally got the blood and tears staunched enough to inspect the damage, we found that he had hit his nose and upper lip on a piece of angle iron sticking out from the bridge.

Aaron had been fishing in the creek, and during the commotion he managed to snag a fishhook in my earlobe. When Patty tried to take it loose, she discovered that the hook was baited with a big wad of well-chewed, pink bubble gum.

Just then, we saw David trotting down the road from their trailer, carrying a little plastic play doctor kit. In all seriousness, he strode up to Jeremy and said soberly, "Here, Brother, I brought my doctor kit!"

No, there's never a dull moment around here. This was

also the week that one of the grandsons dug a hole and buried Poppaw's tractor keys, and someone let my baby mallard ducks out and I haven't seen them since.

After we heard a sermon on husband and wife relationships, I told our pastor that if Criss happens to pass away before I do, I have three main ambitions. I don't want to remarry, I plan to eat at least a cup of garlic every day, and I want to travel. He said he thought I'd covered the whole thing pretty neatly. He commented, "Well, if you eat a cup of garlic every day you definitely won't remarry, and you will be forced to travel as you can't stay in one place very long!"

The men and boys in our family have made some famous trades and bad purchases. Michael started with the famed motorcycle that was motor-less and traded it to his Uncle Cornelius for a pistol held together by a nail. Then he sold the pistol for fifty cents. I think making bad deals is a family trait.

Back in the lean days of our early marriage, Criss bought a car that that had been patched with body putty. Later, he discovered that the holes behind the putty were stuffed full of rags. That may be the car where the floorboard collapsed down through the frame.

He once bought a cow from a fellow that assured him it was a purebred Hereford. A few days of rain later, he found that she had white spots on her face that had been covered with shoe polish. No wonder Mike is such a good trader.

He's not as good as my brother Larry, however. The boys

go to the stock market quite frequently, and Larry bought a fine looking cow with a huge milk sack. After he began milking her, he discovered that in spite of her big sack, she only gave about a pint of milk. In due time, he took her back to the market and sold her.

Later, he was at the stock market again, and spied a beautiful milk cow that looked to be a good milker. He brought her home, and she also gave about a pint of milk. He realized then that he had bought the same cow twice.

There was a shady fellow we knew who stole a cow (this was years ago) and to keep from being found out, he put gumboots on the cow's feet and walked her out of the meadow. (Hillbilly ingenuity?) I don't know if the deed was ever discovered or not.

This is a true story, although the names have been changed to protect the innocent (mainly me!)

Ellie Fay and Pearly June were going to get to go to the big airport at Charleston, and they were plumb excited. "Course Pearly June had been there before with her man Bobby Gene, when they took Aunt Fernie to ketch her plane back to Baltimore. It was a puzzle how them airplanes swallered up people and flew them way up in the sky."

Ellie Fay felt better 'cause Pearly June was going with her. Her and Bobby Gene had learnt all the ropes before. (True, he had put eight quarters in the wrong parking meter, and they had a hard time scratching up enough money to fill the other one.) They only had two hours until Aunt Fernie's plane was s'posed to take off, and they shore didn't want to be late.

Bobby Gene got rattled and left the truck door wide open. When they got back to the truck, Pearly June squalled that they'd been robbed—but the pound of seed corn that they had bought at the farm store was still in there. Bobby Gene got kinda red in the face and confessed that he reckoned he forgot to shet the door.

This time, Ellie Fay's oldest boy, Big Bubba, wuz comin' home on one of them big jets, and they had come to meet him. Ellie Fay couldn't hardly hit the ground with her hat, she wuz that nervous. She was upset driving to Clendenin, and had been to Charleston once or twice, but this airport was all new to her.

When they got there, Pearly June had to git Ellie Fay by the hand and lead her right through the halls—she jist kept a-gawkin' at people. Some of 'em stared at her kinda curious-like, and she couldn't understand why. She had on her best overall jumper and even wore shoes. It mighta been 'cause her babiest boy, Little Bubba, was walkin' so close behind her he was almost plastered to her back.

They watched the people mix and muddle back and forth for awhile as two men in uniform let some of 'em go through a narry alley where a rubber belt swallered up their pocketbooks. Finally, Pearly June got up enough nerve to ask one of the guards, "Hey, whur do people wait fer the planes to come in?"

The tall one motioned fer Ellie Fay to come on through, with Little Bubba hard on her heels. She said she almost jumped out of her hide when a loud buzzer sounded all around her. "Step back!" ordered the guard, and she jumped backwards and stepped on Little Bubba and almost knocked him down.

"Put your hands on your head!" he said sternly. She jist stared at him with her mouth open, and he took her arm and placed her hand on her head. "Now put your other arm on your head!" he ordered. That was enuf fer Ellie Fay. She skittered sideways like a string-haltered horse and screeched, "Don't cha do that to me—I've whupped bigger people than you! Git him, Pearly June, he's gonna frisk me!"

After he calmed her down some, he explained that he only wanted to cover the metal hair clasp on the top of her head. He showed her how the scanner detected metal and even x-rayed the contents of her pocketbook. There musta been a whole lot of people who needed to know this too, fer they stood around listenin' and grinnin'. She shore was glad that she hadn't wore Grandmaw's corset with the steel stays in it.

They had a good time then, waitin' down in the big room fer the plane to come in. Little Bubba had the best time though, runnin' around and tryin' out all them bubble gum machines. Finally, the big airplane came a-zoomin' in. As soon as its wheels touched the ground. Little Bubba hollered, "I see my Bubba!" One of the women a-waitin' there said, "Yes, they're dragging him along behind—I guess his parachute didn't open up!" She musta been a-kiddin' though, 'cause they looked and didn't see nuthin'.

It was shore good to git Big Bubba back home again, with all the plowin' and plantin' that needed to be done. Ellie Fay was afeered that he might have turned into a city slicker, 'specially when he told her how much fun it wuz to ride in an airplane. "Shucks, you ain't a-gittin' me in one of them things," she grumbled. "Iffen the Lord wanted me to fly, he's a-growed wings on me instead of arms!"

Still, she told Pearly June on the way back home, "I reckon we don't git out of the holler enuf!"

Poor Daddy had his share of embarrassments. Mom always used belly bands on her babies, which she carefully ironed after they were laundered. One day someone accidentally put a baby band in the middle of Daddy's freshly ironed handkerchiefs. He was teaching a Sunday school class and pulled out of his pocket what he thought was his hankie. He flourished a baby band in front of the whole class.

That wasn't nearly as bad as the time he wore a pair of brown shoes to church, which were the same color, but one was a slipper and the other a boot. Did I say he was absent-minded?

Criss gets a little confused sometimes too. He dropped a couple of Alka-Seltzer tablets in some warm water the other day and attempted to soak his dentures in it. It didn't do much for his cold, but he has the healthiest teeth in the country.

I have been blessed with a good handyman around the house; it seems as if Criss can do a little bit of everything. He was cutting some trees down for my cousin Debbie and her husband, so I didn't tell her about the sycamore tree that he cut down for us one time. It grew in the edge of our yard, and it must have been taller than Criss had counted on. Anyway, when it came crashing to the ground, it took off my kitchen porch in one fell swoop. He has never lived that down.

One of the redeeming qualities of country people is the ability to laugh at ourselves. We enjoy a good joke on others, and can laugh just as heartily when the joke is on us.

But sometimes jokes have a way of backfiring on you. When our daughter Patty started to high school, one of her teachers was calling the roll and called "Patty Bragg." Stopping there, he inquired jokingly, "Are you related to Fort Bragg?" Without turning a hair, Patty answered seriously, "Yes, he's my uncle." The teacher grew flustered and changed the subject, wondering if she really did have an Uncle Fort. She didn't.

My Uncle Myles was a whole lot like Daddy—absent-mindedness must be an O'Dell trait. I lived with them after I got out of high school and went to work. They had a morning ritual that rarely varied. Aunt Lucy would fix his breakfast and pack his lunch, then go back to bed.

This particular morning he was running a little late, and as he left he grabbed the brown paper sack that Aunt Lucy packed his lunch in. At noon he opened the sack to find the raw sweet potatoes she had purchased at A&P.

I guess this must be hereditary—last night I caught

myself putting a pitcher of Kool-aid in the bathroom shelf instead of the refrigerator.

In bygone years, my sister Mary Ellen grabbed her books one morning and hurried to catch the bus. When she got halfway to school, she discovered that she had the Sears and Roebuck catalog.

After all these years, I still have nightmares about the children catching the school bus in the morning. We used to have 17 youngsters who waited at our house for the "big" bus to run. There was a 20-minute wait after the contract bus ran, and it was too cold during the winter for them to wait outside. I always had a fear that I would find a kid or two left behind after the bus was gone.

I kept a watchful eye out for the bus, and one dark morning I saw approaching lights a few minutes early. I yelled, "Hurry, kids, here comes the bus!" They grabbed their coats, books and assorted gear, streamed out the door and across the bridge, ready to board the bus. It was the garbage truck.

One April Fool's Day my sister Jeannie submitted a column to the county paper which was printed instead of my usual one. She told my life story in lurid detail. She started with my birth: "You were born August 30, 1935—I'll not tell how old you are. You had an extremely warped head, and Daddy thought you were funny-looking. Grandma had delivered you at home and there was no hospital to take you back to, so she finally persuaded Mom to keep you.

"You were so bald that Mom had to put a sock on your head to keep you from freezing to death. (This is true, and for years the name "Sockhead" was always good for a fight!) This was the extremely cold winter down on Big Laurel Creek.

"Before long your parents had presented you with a succession of much better looking brothers and sisters for you to help care for. Your patience with us was amazing. I will never forget you holding my head under water when you washed my hair because I bawled so much.

"Your housekeeping abilities are exceptional. Do you remember the can of upholstery cleaner that went berserk, and in the midst of screaming for help you managed to festoon the walls, floor and ceiling with layers of foam? (I remember!)

"Julia Child should blush with shame over your prowess in the kitchen. There was that memorable eggplant casserole that the dogs wouldn't eat, and did you really bury it with a stake in its heart? And there was that buttermilk pie . . .

"See, I didn't write anything bad. I didn't even mention the time you lost your petticoat on Washington Street during the Christmas rush and Mom ran off and left you— or the time you ran into bank president Murray Smith's parked truck. I don't want to shatter any illusions about you. We love you anyway."

Now who wouldn't laugh?

⋆⇌◎⇋⋆

Did you ever wonder why women have a bad reputation for being poor drivers? I think I've figured it out—I think automobiles hate women drivers. I'm convinced that mine does and I can't understand why. I try to be good to it; I feed it the finest gasoline and get the oil changed regularly. It will get me in a heavy rainstorm, and the windshield wipers won't work.

It will make funny noises when I am backing out, and when my husband checks it, it will purr like a kitten for him. "There is nothing wrong with your car," he tells me. "It must be you." I can almost catch a fleeting grin on the windshield.

For example, a week or so ago, it sneaked around and hid the fact that the state inspection sticker had run out in June. Kevin borrowed it to make a business trip to Charleston, and promptly got a ticket. Criss chewed me out good. "It's your responsibility to take care of the car," he told me. That six on the sticker means it ran out the last of June." I'm almost sure I heard a giggle from the radiator.

It's not just this car either. Every one that I have owned has acted the same way. I had one once that could change its appearance. I went to the grocery store late one evening, and after I purchased my groceries I started to my car with them. It was gone.

Night had fallen, but the parking lot was brightly lit with overhead lights. I circled the lot three times, and it wasn't there. I was in a panic. I ran back inside and told my sister-in-law Alice that someone had stolen my car. "I knew I was going to leave my keys in the switch one time too many," I moaned. "Criss will kill me."

She went out and helped me search for it just to make sure it was really gone. "We'll just have to get Larry to call the state police," she told me. Then she looked across the parking lot again and asked, "Alyce Faye, is that not your car parked over there?" Sure enough, that dratted car had changed its color. "Please don't tell Larry, I begged. I can laugh at myself, but I didn't want Larry laughing.

Then I had an old car that balked on me at the Dollar Store parking lot, and absolutely refused to start. An obliging gentleman who was parked next to me checked my battery terminals and tried to start it with his jumper cables. Nothing. I had to call Andy, who was working at Foodland, to come to my aid. He also checked my battery, and when he leaned on the hood the car drifted a few inches.

"Mommy," he asked suspiciously, "Do you have the car in park?" (Well, it was almost, but not quite.) As soon as I shifted it in park, it roared to life. That car would have never acted that way for a man. I wonder if I am too old to ride a bicycle.

It's house-cleaning time again, and I am having a hard time. How do you clean a house when every member is a collector? I've come to the conclusion that I don't clean out junk—I merely rearrange it. Matthew is the worst of the bunch. What can you do with a kid that saves even the string from his gift packages?

I believe that he is a throwback to Grandpa O'Dell. Now there was a pack rat! Grandpa had an old metal trunk where he stored his treasures. He kept everything—

pieces of string, scrap metal, old shoestrings, worn-out shoe heels, bent nails, and dozens of combs (we couldn't keep a comb, for some reason, they all mysteriously disappeared.)

He kept it locked, and every time he opened it, we children would crowd around Grandpa's knees to see his carefully hoarded treasures. "Now you kids don't plunder in that stuff," he would say testily. We would stand back respectfully as he lifted the flat tray from the top to search for something he needed—or to stash another treasure away. The trunk had a peculiar, metallic odor that I can smell yet today.

I believe I have the answer to my dilemma. We need to find an old metal trunk like Grandpa's for Matthew to store his treasures. But I wonder if you can find one that measures twelve feet by twelve feet?

Patty and Randy have been away for a few days visiting relatives in Ohio. On their way home, they got lost on the back streets of one town with a luggage rack full of bicycles, toys, high chair, etc. (You have to know Patty to understand what she packs for an overnight visit.) They circled around and passed the same group of people three times. Of course by this time they were an object of attention.

Patty waved and spoke to them. Randy sort of fussed to her about speaking to strangers, but she explained, "I kinda feel like I know them, Randy—we've passed them so many times!"

That reminds me of the time when we moved home from Jackson County, right before Kevin was born. We had an old pick-up truck held together with prayer and baling wire, and in the back were nearly all of our worldly possessions. (Talk about being hard up!) We had a dozen chickens in a homemade crate made with poles, two bushels of grapes, baskets of clothes, and two hound dogs tied to the rack.

My sister Susie was with us, and we had Mike and Patty in the cab of the truck also. Our truck wouldn't idle, and had a bad habit of quitting on us when we braked. It was high noon when we reached the town of Spencer, and well-dressed people were strolling the sidewalks, coming home from church.

Criss was praying. "Please, Lord, don't let us hit a red light!" Naturally, the light turned red just as we reached it, right in the middle of town. Criss stepped on the brake, and the truck sputtered and quit. The chickens stuck their heads out between the poles, the hound dogs trailed their ears over the tailgate, and Criss got redder and redder. There we sat, as heads turned to stare at us. (The Beverly Hillbillies were not in the race!)

Finally some kind Samaritan had mercy on us and gave us a push from behind, and we were on our way. I was afraid to say a word, but a few miles out of town Criss burst out laughing and we all exploded. Susie has never forgotten our trip home, and neither have we.

Nicholas made his daily trip down to visit (sometimes two or three) and picked up a pot holder that Patty had made for me. It was decorated with large purple flowers, and it caught his eye. "Can I take this home with me?" he asked. I had been using it all day. So I told him I had a new one just like it that he could have. He took the new one and the well-used one as well.

On the way home his curious mother asked, "Why did you want that dirty pot holder?" He held it up to his nose, sniffed with satisfaction, and then answered, "It smells just like Mommaw!

My cousin Rex was reminiscing about the summer that he and his brother Bernard spent visiting Grandpa and Grandma O'Dell on this very farm. They made themselves slingshots and gathered pebbles from the creek for their ammunition. They started on a hunting trip out through the garden, when a couple of "things" flew up with a loud flutter.

The young boys bore down with their trusty weapons, and brought down their game. They proudly carried their trophies to the house, but Grandma wasn't too happy—they had killed her two prize banty chickens. (Grandpa thought it was funny—I can hear him wheezing and laughing now.) She took the boys to the woodshed and gave them a good old country licking.

I guess that Grandma had never heard that corporal punishment could warp the boys' self-esteem, and I'm sure she never heard of a "time out." She went by the Bible admonition of "Spare the rod and spoil the child." Cousin Rex says that at 82 years of age, he can still feel the sting!

One night I took out my lower dentures and slipped

them underneath my pillow because my gums were sore. The next morning I forgot them under my pillow and got up to cook breakfast. When I went in to wake up Criss, he was sitting up in bed with a very foolish look on his face. Seems that he had roused up, found my teeth, and thought he had lost his in the night. Still half asleep, he was trying to fit my lower dentures on top of his own.

One spring we had what I now call "The Great Cow Manure Battle." We had four strapping boys, but the youngest, Matthew, seemed to get into more trouble. That year Criss had just painted the barn a bright red that simply gleamed. Matthew and a few of his friends, namely cousins Eric Perdue and Noel Braley, plus Jeff Braley and Tony Bullard, were playing around the barn. When I pressed Matthew for details, he answered, "I don't know, Mom—that was 30 years ago!" That may be true, but the evidence is still there.

They must have been bored. They began tossing dried cow chips at the barn, and soon they were throwing them at one another. It evolved into fresher cow patties, and the battle grew heated. Matthew picked up one that was pretty soupy, just as Jeff stuck his head up and hollered. He got a mouthful.

He was crying, and they took him down to the creek and washed him off, begging him all the time not to tell. I don't know how they could keep it a secret. I had to take Tony to the washhouse for a shower, and then find him clean clothes. Criss now had a red barn with black polka dots, which was no secret.

Search *Home and Garden* from cover to cover, and there are no hints on how to clean a barn. I did read how to give your home a "country" look. You simply lean a hoe, rake, etc. in the corner of the living room. We've had a country look for years. Sometimes the corner of the living room is decorated with a sack of grass seed ("I'm going to move that—I didn't want it to get wet!") There are always hunting guns, game bags, camouflage outfits and hunting boots. How country can you get?

This same magazine author recommended putting your beloved articles to a practical use. "Use a lovely evening bag for a candy dish." In the first place, I don't have a lovely evening bag—would an old toboggan do as well?

Patty got ready for her 10-year high school reunion, and it was a scramble to get three little boys looking presentable. "Mom," she moaned, "Adrian fell and skinned his nose, and you know Luke cut his hair. If I could have seen this ten years ago, I probably would have hunted me a deep cave and crawled in. Wonder what ten more years will bring?" (The years now have brought her five grandchildren and another on the way.)

Tuesday was one of those 3-H days (hazy, hot, and humid); Murphy's Law prevailed from the very beginning. The first thing I did was get my pantyhose wound up in the fan. It wasn't as bad as it sounds—I was coming through the kitchen with a basket of clean laundry, and dropped them on the top of one of those old-fashioned fans, which promptly devoured them and stalled. I got excited and unplugged the typewriter, which didn't help a bit.

It reminded me of the time that nephew Bruce was visiting here and something funny happened. Bruce laughed hysterically and gasped, "That's the funniest thing I've seen since Aunt Rade got her shorts caught in the mixer. I didn't ask him the details.

There is a saying that goes: Eavesdroppers never hear good of themselves. Sometimes it doesn't pay to listen in. Criss and Patty were having a conversation in the living room while I was puttering around in the kitchen, and I couldn't help but hear them.

"Mommy told Jennifer that she got around real good at the store today," laughed Patty. (Here I need to explain that Patty agreed to take me to the grocery store if I would use one of those motorized carts provided for handicapped people. It was after I'd broken my leg and she was afraid it would be too hard for me to limp around on my walker.)

I was hesitant, as I'd never learned to drive an ATV, but she talked me into it. I really thought that I had maneuvered the electric cart up and down the aisles in fine style.

Patty continued, "You should have seen her. She almost ran over the same man three times, and the clerks had to move one of the displays so she could get through." (Actually, I had run up on a pallet and couldn't go any farther.)

Criss started laughing. "Did I ever tell you about the time we went to Wal-Mart and she ran over a lady?" he asked. (I tried to hide behind the refrigerator.) "She had a big lug in her basket (no, it wasn't Criss) and couldn't see over the top of it. There was a lady stooped down looking at a card display on a lower rack and Mommy hit her in the rump and bowled her over."

She was the nicest lady—she apologized to me! She said she shouldn't have been down in the floor like that, and that it was her own fault. I kept telling her how sorry I was. The Lord must have been watching over me. She could have sued me, sued the store, or clobbered me over the head with her purse. Criss didn't tell Patty that he disappeared, and I didn't see him until I checked out.

Then the talk drifted to my ability to drive a car. Now, there are lots of things I don't tell Criss unless he asks. After all, silence is golden, is it not? I think some of the things the kids spilled were news to him. Patty started it. "Boy, it was so funny when Mommy backed into the backhoe. She hit it so hard that it just went ker-thump. Mom Granny looked up and asked mildly. "Did we hit something?"

Criss looked as if he had been pole-axed between the eyes. I tried to justify myself. "Well, it was parked in brother Butch's driveway. Nobody ever parks there. I didn't look back; I just backed up." Patty made it worse. "Mom," she said. "You did it twice!"

Criss had to add to his growing list of my misadventures. "You know, there was a big damaged place on the church siding, sort of high up, and I couldn't figure out what had caused it. One day I had the ton truck up there, and I started measuring. Sure enough, the damaged place was exactly the same height as my truck bed. I got suspicious.

"I came home and asked Alyce Faye, "Did you by any chance run the ton truck into the church? She squirmed around a little bit and stammered, 'Well, I could have—I thought I might have. I wasn't sure.' Well, I was sure."

This was getting worse. I had a feeling I was about to get my license revoked. They began reaching 'way back in the past and dragging out things that should have been long forgotten.

Criss was getting into rare form. He continued, "Did I ever tell you about the time she was taking the car to the body shop to get it fixed?" he asked. Mike had run the church bus into the car and dented the door, so I sent her to the body shop.

"It was raining cats and dogs, so I was knocked off from work. As I was coming home, I see this car sideways in the road, with the front end against the guardrail. It had just wrecked. As I got closer I saw it was Alyce Faye."

Was it ever raining! I was coming down the river road when all at once the car began hydroplaning. I couldn't do a thing with it—it was all over the road. When I finally got stopped, I had smashed the front end into the guardrail. I had a song tape in the player and it was still playing, "I Have My Hand in the Hand of the Lord." He surely did have His hand over me.

When the first vehicle approached and I saw it was Criss, I cringed. I thought, "Boy, I've had it now!" He didn't say a word, but told the fellow with him to take his truck on home. He got in the car, started it, and headed for the body shop. All at once he started laughing. "What's so funny?" I asked. "That's the funniest thing I ever heard," he replied. "You had a wreck on your way to the body shop!"

I will never live that one down.

It probably didn't help my image when my fifteen-year-old grandson David and I had an ATV accident a couple of years ago and I fractured my back. I mean, how gracefully can you land when you shoot straight up in the air and come down hard on your posterior? Come to think about it, the metal brace that I had to wear for six months wasn't too elegant either.

Mom is not a bit of help. She stopped me in the supermarket the other day and straightened up my coat collar. I wasn't shocked, just rather surprised that she didn't take out her hankie and spit wash my face. She is still trying, after all these years, to make a lady out of me.

As hard as I try, I can't cultivate a tinkling little laugh. My brother Larry and I both inherited a hearty belly laugh from Daddy, which sometimes rolls out at inappropriate moments. This must have passed down to our son Mike, along with other traits.

One time my sister Susie, Mike and I sang at an old-fashioned wake held in the deceased's home. We sang until well after midnight, and then the old man's grandson walked with us to our truck and thanked us gratefully. Mike told him cheerily, "Oh, you're welcome—we had a ball!" Susie and I managed to get inside the truck before we collapsed, laughing hysterically.

Night falls softly on another mild October day, leaving mauve and lavender streaks in the western sky with a misty new moon rising. It has been another satisfying autumn day; the leaves dry and crunchy underfoot and the air warm and balmy. In weather such as this, Daddy used to take us to Hickory Knob for camp outs.

After the grandchildren started coming, he would insist on all of them going too. I remember one particular time when we were camped at Ha'nted Lick, and all of Daddy's grandchildren were there. The older grandsons, Mike, Kevin, Andy, Danny, Freddie and Doug were encased in sleeping bags in a row around the campfire, and the rest of the brood, including Mom and Daddy, were stuffed in a tent close by.

Daddy was getting older then, and he was tired and sleepy. The boys kept getting louder and rowdier, with much laughing and giggling. He warned them to be still several times, and then he threatened, "If I have to tell you again, I'm going to get up and smack your jaws!"

Of course they kept on, and Daddy slipped up and carried out his threat. In the flickering firelight, he got a little mixed up and cuffed Freddie twice, and Andy got by scot-free. Naturally, that did set them off, and they laughed and carried on until sleep finally overtook them. It remains one of their cherished memories to this day.

⊶⊷⊷⊶

Our huge, heavy piano in the living room is gasping out its last breath, and we have to do something with it. It took four men and an elephant to move it in, but who wants to leave a dead piano underfoot?

We finally laid it peacefully to rest—at least, I hope it doesn't come back to haunt us. Matthew and I finally managed to get it as far as the front door—did you ever see anything as heavy as one of those old-time pianos? We couldn't get it across the threshold. Matthew gave a mighty heave to the top of it (it was hinged) and promptly gave himself a solid wallop on the cheekbone. I'm afraid I laughed.

Kevin came along and helped lift it across the sill. After he got it on the porch, he thought it would be fun to give it a great push out into the yard. It took off a bit faster than he had anticipated, and almost took a porch column with it. (I'm telling you, this thing had a life of its own!) Naturally, it splattered on its back in the yard, so Criss got the backhoe to scoop it up.

As he was working the levers, trying furiously to get a grip on the dead monster, Randy came by. He stood watching for a minute, and then remarked, "Why, he'll never play the piano with that thing!"

While all the boys were here, they were pressured into going after Sarah's piano to replace the disabled one. Later, one of the neighbors said she saw a pickup truck coming from Kevin and Sarah's house with a piano in the back and a couple of Laurel and Hardy types (Mike and Kevin) playing the piano and singing at the top of their lungs. It was a circus from start to finish.

They backed the truck up against the porch, and attempted to strong arm the piano off the back. I heard Kevin moaning and looked down to see him writhing and groaning on the ground. It seemed he had stepped off the porch with one leg and had skinned the same from knee to ankle. We finally got the thing safely ensconced in the corner where it sits, alive and waiting. The boys made some dire threats if they ever have to move it again.

My sister Jeannie had an old piano in her basement that had expired, and she took a different approach. She decided it would be easier to take it out in pieces, so Sister Jeannie "took an axe and gave her piano forty whacks." Unfortunately, she started at the bottom and worked up. Naturally, when she cut the legs out from under it, it fell down on her head, leaving her wounded and bleeding.

She was there alone, so she staggered out the door and made her way down the road, coming to my house. One of the gas men picked her up and brought her to my door. (I hope she wasn't still carrying the axe.) There stood this bedraggled, bloody creature, with blood still streaming down her face all the way to the hem of her dress.

Alarmed, I led her to the bathroom and cleaned her up to find several superficial cuts on her scalp. I'm so glad we didn't take an axe to our piano.

When my youngest sister Susie was visiting Jeannie after she had moved out of state, she decided one day to go shopping. She parked her car in a parking lot and went in one of the stores there. She came back out, unlocked her car, and drove away. As she drove along, she noticed an unfamiliar object hanging on the rearview mirror. "Hmmmm" she muttered to herself, "I don't remember putting those newspapers in the backseat either."

She opened the glove compartment and realized, "This is not my car!" She hurriedly turned around and drove back to the parking lot to find an irate man pacing around her car. She tried to explain that the cars were identical, and her key did fit. He was not a happy camper.

My brother Ronnie made a beautiful faux pas when they lived in Louisiana. They lived in an apartment complex that was built around a swimming pool, and the apartments were all identical. Uncle Myles and Aunt Lucille had an apartment there also. One day, Ronnie swam in the pool for a while, then wandered into Aunt Lucille's apartment for something to eat.

No one was there, so he rummaged around in the refrigerator and took out the makings for a sandwich. He poured himself a glass of milk and sat down to relax and eat. An older lady came in and sat down. Thinking she was one of Aunt Lucille's friends, he asked her if she wanted a sandwich.

She politely declined his offer, and then he asked her if she was looking for Aunt Lucille. "No," she answered with a small grin, "I live here!" He was in the wrong apartment.

Our youngest daughter Crystal was so particular with her first baby, Alyssa, that she flipped when I fed her a graham cracker. She was about five months old at the time. I didn't get too perturbed as I remembered my first one, Michael. I measured out his baby food by the teaspoonful.

When her second one, Brionna, came along, she was much more relaxed. (Sometimes I think you practice on the first one!) She called us one day to tell us what Bree had eaten as she foraged around the house. Two lady beetles (dead or alive; she didn't say), a green tomato, an ear of raw corn, two cooked ears, and some blackberries. She thrived on it.

⋆⇒◯⇐⋆

I think Ronnie must have inherited his genes from Daddy. This happened during "The War" when many things were rationed, and other items were scarce, including ladies' underclothing. Mom and Daddy were browsing in a five and ten-cent store in Charleston, and Daddy spied a counter of women's panties. Unknown to Daddy, Mom had moved a couple of aisles away and was looking at something else.

Daddy held up an enormous pair of panties and exclaimed loudly to the lady beside him (whom he thought was Mom), "Look here, Delphia—here you can get you some bloomers!" It wasn't Delphia, but a strange lady who was quite plump. Mom loved it. I don't know if the fat lady did or not.

⋆⇒◯⇐⋆

Many years ago while we were in the paving business, we got a job application from my nephew, Eric. It was handwritten and read like this: "Dear Mr. Bragg, I am actively seeking employment and not only that, I am looking for a job. You will be able to tell from the following information that I am well qualified for a position in your establishment.

"1. I have talked to Shorty Braley at length about the finer aspects of paving. He very knowingly explained what 'chip and tar' means.

"2. I have memorized every lever on the paver, Lever A and Lever B. If I can't figure out Lever A, I'll try Lever B.

"3. I once drove by on the interstate and saw the entire procedure.

"4. I am able to fall up the stairs every evening or if the situation demands it, I can trip over a crack in the sidewalk and break my dinner bucket—preferable at high noon at the state capitol.

"5. I like old model Ford trucks, Norwegian squirrel dogs, and fat women, and I don't believe in brown-nosing, Mr. Criss, sir.

"6. I will accept anything from minimum wage on up. But I can't work for less than $4 per hour.

"As you can see, my credentials are faultless. If hired, I will show you my secret merkle (morel) patch.

"Very sincerely, truly, appreciatively, lovingly, Your most loving nephew, Eric Perdue

"PS. I like your nose. I always have."

(I should clarify that Eric wasn't referring to his wife Vicki when he mentioned "fat women." He wasn't even married at the time. Of course he meant me, his fat Aunt Alyce Faye.)

Our daughter Crystal is not immune to a few blunders herself. She had gone to a fancy dinner and came home late that evening. She came in her house, remembered she had left some dishes of food in the car and kicked off her high-heeled shoes. Jeff's work boots were handy beside the door, so she slipped her feet into them. Not taking time to tie the shoelaces, she clumped to the car and came back through the door with her arms laden with dishes of food.

As the door closed behind her, it also shut on her trailing shoelaces and she fell headlong into the entry— still clutching her dishes. She moaned and groaned and declared she had broken her foot. Jeff was at a fireman's meeting and she was alone with the girls. When Jeff came home, she was having chills, so he took her to the emergency room. She waited for two painful hours without seeing a doctor.

Finally she told Jeff, "Just take me home and I'll die a natural death." I don't know what the moral of the story is, unless it is to be sure and tie your shoelaces if you are going to wear your husband's work shoes.

I may have had my moments in driving a car, but I never did wreck a horse. Criss did. A few years back, he acquired a nice black mare and saddled her up to take a ride. He was sitting high in the saddle as he took a test drive up the "little road" past our house. She r'ared up with him, and he pulled on the reins, jerking up her head. Of course that was the wrong thing to do, as she overbalanced and fell on her back in the ditch line. He came leading her back, his face as white as a sheet. That was the first time I'd ever heard of wrecking a horse in a ditch.

You would think he had learned his lesson. A couple of years ago, he decided to ride his beautiful black mare (this was another horse) in the Golden Delicious Apple Festival parade. He shined up both himself and Black Beauty, and attired in a red-checked cowboy shirt and white hat, he took his place proudly in the parade.

He looked so handsome as the horse pranced down the street, and all went well until the parade turned and came back the opposite direction. Unfortunately, they met a line of motorcyclists, and one wise guy gunned his motor just as he met Black Beauty and his rider. She rose straight up on her hind legs and would have fallen backward on a car behind them if Criss hadn't gone through this before.

My brother Larry was standing beside a fellow on the sidewalk watching them, and the man remarked, "That old man sure knows how to ride a horse!" Patty was right behind Criss on her horse and she yelled, "Heck, that old man is just trying to stick on!"

Things went pretty well on up the street, until they came to the amusement rides. Just as they went by, one of the big motors roared to life. Black Beauty again stood up on her hind legs, and Criss swore that she walked that way for at least ten feet. We are wondering if he plans to be in the parade this year. I reckon he'll never learn—he acquired another black mare just the other day.

We kept Mom in our home for over three years, and then our dog knocked me down and broke my leg. My sisters tried to take care of her, but being sick themselves, they were not able. Thank the Lord for Dovie's Retirement Home. Dovie took Mom in and treated her like her own mother, and soon Mom settled in and thought she was home.

Before my leg had healed, I had to undergo gall bladder

surgery, and then I had bleeding ulcers. By then, I wouldn't have moved Mom if I had been able to take care of her. When I visited her, sometimes she would say, "I think I'll go home with you." By the time I was ready to leave, she had changed her mind and wanted to stay there.

One day Dovie had some problems with her air conditioning system (lightning had run in on it) and called a repairman to fix it. He was a nice looking young man, and as he worked he noticed Mom struggling to get up off the couch. He went over and got her arms and pulled her up. Then he asked, "Now where did you want to go?" With a sneaky grin she told him, "Just anywhere you want to take me!"

※━◦◠━※

In a family our size, we are bound to have some accidents. Some of them are downright weird. Crystal has been sporting a big black eye for over a week. A bed fell on her. No, she wasn't under the bed; it was the top bunk in a camper. Crystal and three of her friends decided to spend the night in my sister Susie's camper which was parked in Mom's yard.

About one o'clock in the morning, her friend Lori climbed up on the top bunk while Crystal was bedded down in the bottom one. For some reason, the top bunk pulled loose from the ceiling and crashed down on Crystal's head. To keep from alarming me, they didn't call me from Mom's until the next morning.

When I walked in church and saw her, I was stunned. She looked like Mom's old cat when it got its head caught in a steel trap. Thank goodness, Crystal had no permanent damage. The cat survived also.

My sister Susie can make short work of clutter. Even as a kid, she knew exactly what to do. One time she cleaned my house when my own children were small. She picked up everything that was laying loose—books, toys, shoes, clean clothes, dirty clothes, etc. and piled them in the baby bed. She then covered the whole mess with a lovely quilt.

It looked fine, except Criss couldn't find his work shoes, and the baby didn't have anywhere to sleep.

Treeing the Coon and Outsmarting the Trout

Summer brings maturity to our hills, with the trees festooned with full-grown leaves and the earth rampant with growth. It is a busy time, with crops and gardens to tend, but soon harvest comes and summer is over. The cycle begins once again.

I love the people of these hills, stubbornly clinging to our hillside farms and windy ridges—plain spoken, sturdy people who are still working the land that their fathers and grandfathers worked before them. People who are satisfied with a warm home in winter and a garden patch to till in the summer. People happy to have a good coon dog to hunt in the fall and a squirrel dog for squirrel season. Most of all, happy to be free—free to worship God, free to come and go. We are a blessed people. This is home, and I love it.

Hunting is a way of life here in the hills, and our boys start early. When our late neighbor Gerald Braley was a young lad, he attended Hagar Grade School. He loved to hunt, and came to school one day smelling strongly of the skunk he had encountered the night before. Exasperated, the teacher asked him, "Gerald, make up your mind. Do you want to hunt or go to school?" Quick as a wink, Gerald replied, "That ain't no decision a'tall!" He never looked back.

There is a sequel to this story. Years later, Gerald worked with Criss in the asphalt paving business. One day they were grading a large lot, and pushing the dirt over the hill until it formed a 50-foot slope. Gerald got too near the edge and fell down the slope, scooting headfirst on his belly. About halfway down, his descent slowed and he yelled suddenly, "Hey—there's a coon track!"

His father, Dick Braley, trapped during the winter and shipped the hides out of state. The firm that received the hides hired a new fur grader, and he got much less for the last shipment of hides than he had been receiving. He wrote a scorching letter to the company, adding that "he didn't have no hides for a greenhorn to spearmint on." Yes, our people are plainspoken.

Hunting season is here in full force, and I hear a lot of hunting tales. Andy and Bruce Belt were up in Dog Run country the other night, and they treed a coon. What makes this tale different, however, was the fact they didn't have a dog with them.

Andy left Bruce at the tree while he went after his gun, and while he was gone, the coon tried to come down. Bruce had to bark several times to keep the coon up the tree, and when Andy returned he was still barking treed. They got the coon. Who needs a dog when Bruce is around?

One of the funniest accidents we had was when Andy built a snare. He has always been a frustrated woodsman—he was born about 200 years too late. He would have fit in perfectly during the Daniel Boone era. When he was just a young lad, Matthew was his loyal sidekick. One lazy Sunday afternoon, he decided to take Matthew up in the woods and build a wild animal snare.

I don't know what kind of a wild animal he planned to trap in the woods of Clay County, but he had high hopes. He bent a couple of supple saplings over and fashioned a snare with a loop of rope and a large rock anchoring it. The idea was, when an unsuspecting animal came running by (or hopping, slinking, crawling, etc.,) it would stick its neck or foot in the loop of rope, the trap would spring, and the hapless animal would be suspended up in the air.

He worked diligently, fashioning the snare until it suited him perfectly. He looked upon it with satisfaction, and then decided to test it. He stuck his toe gingerly in the trap, and it was successful beyond his wildest expectations. Before you could say "Hiss, cat," and in front Matthew's astonished eyes, the trap went "sloop" and Andy was hanging by one leg from the top of the sapling.

I don't know how Matthew managed to get him down, but he brought him to the house torn and bleeding, and a little reluctant to discuss the matter. He carries scars on his face yet today. It was almost as bad as the time they built a tree house, and it fell down with them in it.

⊷⇒◉⇐⊶

My nephew Noel does a lot of coon hunting up in Jackson

County, and he wrote me a poem the other day that goes like this:

> *I got a coon dog by the name of Big Joe,*
> *He's fast enough to catch a coon by the toe.*
> *When I let him loose, I heard a squall,*
> *Next time I heard him, he was east of Omaha.*
> *When I looked up the big oak tree,*
> *There sat a coon as big as me.*
> *Well, I shined my light right into his eyes,*
> *And over his back sat a coon twice that size.*
> *I shot him out, and the fur was good,*
> *But I had to stretch the hide upon a car hood.*

I thought the poem was good, and told him so. His mother Susie then told him he ought to tell me about skinning the skunk in the wheelbarrow, and then filling it up with wood for the stove. I don't think he was very popular around the house for a while.

Turkey season is here, and Andy has been practicing his turkey calls until he can hardly speak English. He let Kevin try one out, and then laughed hysterically at the strange noises Kevin made. His eyes bulged, his face turned red, and the cords in his neck stood out. Criss finally told him that he doubted if a turkey would respond, but he could probably steal chickens!

My week has been tinged with a touch of sadness. We let Sam, Matthew's purebred Treeing Walker coonhound, go to a new home. He was really mine, and considered me his private property. Matthew had discovered Tammy, but decided he'd rather court than coon hunt. It wasn't fair to a dog of Sam's caliber to keep him tied and not hunt him.

Nevertheless, when I passed his doghouse this morning, there was no seventy-five pounds of joyous dog to greet me happily; no soft, wet nose thrust into my hand. There was an empty chain lying on the ground, and my heart felt empty too. Aaron told Patty that "they took old Sam, and Mommaw didn't even get to kiss him goodbye."

Mike and Peggy are packing their camper to take their three little ones to Williams River for a few days of fishing and relaxing. When six-year-old David heard of their plans, he ran through the house and shouted, "Oh, boy, we can go bear hunting!" Then he turned and added, "But I sure hope we don't find any!"

Andy has been bow hunting for deer the past few days, so far without success. He did construct himself an ingenious tree stand, and came in to show it off with it strapped proudly on his back. He looked exactly like Darius Green and his Flying Machine—a good stiff wind could have picked him up and sailed him off into the wild blue yonder.

When we finished laughing at it, Kevin did admit that it would probably work just fine if he could find a square tree to use it on. Andy retorted, "Go ahead and laugh—you'll be laughing out of the other side of your mouth when I come dragging my big deer in!" He was right about one thing—if he turned it over and used it like a sled, it would be perfect to haul a deer in. We really do appreciate Andy. It's not every family who has an inventor in its ranks.

⬦═◉═⬦

The boys begin hunting young here in the hills, where wild game is a fact of life. Most country families have a rabbit beagle, a squirrel dog, and sometimes a coon dog as well. Criss got a beagle pup from his brother the other day, which we dubbed "Clyde." Clyde hasn't figured out just exactly what a beagle is supposed to do. Andy took him out hunting with his beagle dog, and they both started out energetically.

In a little while Andy heard Clyde barking—he has a deep "arooo-arooo" bark that is quite distinctive. Andy thought with satisfaction. "Boy, old Clyde is putting one around the mountain." Then he realized that the barking was all coming from one spot. When he investigated, he found Clyde tangled up in a brier patch, barking piteously. He had to carry the pup out in his arms. The next time he saw Clyde, he was sleeping sweetly on a rug on my front porch.

I started through the yard a few days ago, and a wild rabbit bounded around the garage and met Clyde head-on. He didn't glance toward the rabbit but kept coming toward me as the rabbit ran up the hill. Criss says he has the makings of a real rabbit dog, but he is still just a baby. He'll get lined out if he can ever conquer the brier patches.

⬦═◉═⬦

Dogs and hunting are a way of life here in the hills. I can never remember a time when we didn't have hunting dogs, and just plain dogs. Great attachments are made between man, and man's best friend. A young fellow told Criss some time ago about a dog he owned. "He's half collie, half Norwegian, and half husky," he said proudly. "Steve," Criss answered, "You don't have a dog; you have a dog and a half!" Steve laughed and agreed that it was so.

Someone told my brother-in-law Jim about a dog they owned—a Government Pincher (Doberman pinscher)! I know all about those government pinchers. They pinch us around April 15 each year.

I heard a good hunting tale recently, but I can't name names. A certain older man and his nephew were at a fishing camp, and the older man, who had been out of state, was hankering for a good mess of venison. (It was not deer season.) They decided to go spotlighting (another crime) as it was in an isolated spot and they were not in danger of getting caught.

They took two powerful flashlights and took off through the woods. Sure enough, they spotted a nice, fat doe and dispatched her. They skinned her out right there in the woods, and started back to the camp, carrying the fresh meat on their shoulders. The older man stuck his flashlight in his hip pocket and followed his nephew through the woods.

The younger man looked behind them and saw a spotlight shining behind them. "Run," he yelled excitedly. "The game warden is after us!" It was some time before they realized that his uncle had accidentally turned on his spotlight and it was shining out of his back pocket.

February came in a mild and gentle fashion, and gave us a week of beautiful spring-like weather. The unseasonable warmth has melted all the accumulation of snow and the ground is bare and brown once more. The jagged columns of icicles have melted from the rock cliffs, and only a few untidy, mushy heaps remain. The creek runs swift and muddy, and we hear again the hopeful melody of a songbird. The hills stretch and yawn in the warm sunshine, but doubtless will sleep once more clasped in the frigid arms of winter.

Randy and Matthew decided to take advantage of one of these warm nights, and took their dogs out coon hunting. The season was limited to the training of the dogs, so they left their firearms at home. They took Old Blue, a seasoned coon hound and Zeke, Randy's young Treeing Walker. They turned the dogs loose at the mouth of one of Elk River's many hollers, and they tore up the steep mountainside with coon on their minds.

At least it was on Old Blue's mind; Zeke probably went along just for the ride. In just a little while they heard Old Blue strike a hot track. They struggled up the side of the steep mountain, warm breezes blowing around their heads. It was a delightful night, with the air cool and brisk close to the river, but warm and balmy higher on the mountain. They could hear Old Blue as he climbed the steep hill, went down the other side, crossed the swift branch, and started up the mountain on the other side.

Randy and Matthew tore through the brush, encouraging Zeke, and reveling in the warm night air. Randy has a bum foot, but he manfully toiled up the steep river slope, trying to keep up with Matthew and Zeke, who by now had gotten into the spirit of the game. High on the mountain they heard Old Blue bark, "treed." Zeke ran ahead and both dogs were barking up a tall white oak when the boys arrived.

They could see a big furry object crouched on a limb—it was a large coon. It totally ignored the boys and the dogs. They threw a few pebbles to get its attention, all to no avail. Finally Matthew squalled like a coon (he said) and the animal turned and looked right into their hunting lights. Old Blue went wild, and so did Randy. He was encouraging Zeke to bark, so Randy patted the tree and "sic'ed" Zeke onward.

Randy even barked himself (more like a blue tick hound, Matthew said) but he didn't try to chew the bark. They weren't getting anywhere, so they decided to leave. They snapped the leash on Old Blue and started back down the mountainside. Instead of going back down the steep slope, they followed the stream back to the mouth of the holler where they had parked the truck.

Matthew went ahead, with Randy and Zeke following, slipping and sliding. Mountains on each side were so steep that they had to traverse the streambed. The water was shallow, but icy cold with the melting snow that fed it. They reached a stretch where the streambed was solid bedrock, covered with moss and quite slippery. Randy was plodding along behind, carefully picking his way with his bad foot.

Matthew heard a tremendous splash, like a bear had come out of hibernation and stumbled in the water. He looked around to find Randy spread-eagled on his back in the cold running water. The water was running from the back of his head to the heels of his shoes. Finally he wallowed around and got to his feet. Matthew couldn't assist him, as he was laughing too hard. He resumed his slogging, watery way behind Matthew, shoes squishing with each step.

After an eternity, they reached the truck and started home. Randy sighed thankfully and sank back in the seat, wet and cold. (Maybe I should explain here that the gas gauge doesn't work on Matthew's truck, and you have to guess how much gas you have.) Up Dulls Creek Mountain the truck began an ominous sputtering. Randy muttered between clenched, chattering teeth, "Matthew, if you are out of gas, I will kill you!"

He was. They managed to coast the truck back down the hill, and sat outside Dan Walker's house, arguing about who was going in to make a telephone call for help. Poor Randy lost, and he had to drag his cold, wet body out of the truck to call home. It was long distance, and he offered Mr. Walker all the money he had for the call—which was 74 cents. Mr. Walker laughed and told him to give the money to Matthew for gasoline. For some reason, Randy hasn't been too enthused about going hunting with Matthew now.

⋯⋙◉◑⋙⋯

My ex-son-in-law Randy and nephew Noel got lost once in the deep, dark woods of Jackson County. It came a pouring-down rain in the middle of the night, and they lost their bearings while searching for the truck. They wandered aimlessly the rest of the night, wet and miserable. Randy had a hunting pistol strapped to his belt, and he attempted to crawl under an electric fence. He got the gun entangled in the fence, and being soaked to the skin, almost electrocuted himself.

When daylight came, they found they had circled the truck all night long. That was a hunting trip they still remember. Getting lost is bad enough, but to get lost, waterlogged and then shocked out of your hunting boots is too much.

Most of us have memories of certain snowstorms that stand out in our minds. My brother Larry had a recent experience that he will remember for a long time. It was the first day of buck season, and he took two of his grandsons, Jamie and Joey, with their father Jim to his camp at the head of Gauley.

Jim shot a buck and wounded it. The boys went back to camp, but Jim and Larry proceeded to track it down the South Fork and back up the Middle Fork. Afternoon wore on and evening came, and the going got rougher and rougher. There was about 30 inches of snow on the ground, and sometimes they were floundering around through snow-laden brush and tops of fallen trees where the drifts were almost waist high.

Larry got concerned that dark was going to catch them, and asked Jim if he wanted to give it up and go back to camp. Jim replied that the deer had the most enormous set of horns on him, and he couldn't bear to quit. They came out on a ridge just as it began to get dusk, and there were bear tracks all around. Larry suggested finding a sheltered rock, building a fire, and spending the night there.

With a quick look behind him at the bear tracks, Jim replied, "Ain't no way!" So on they trudged, through snow, brambles and brush, with Jim frequently casting quick looks behind him. It was a welcome sight, when about nine o'clock that night, they saw Jamie holding a light above his head near the camp. The trophy buck was probably the farthest thing from Jim's mind right then.

Fishing is as important to us as hunting. Early spring finds us camping on a trout stream, and fish and ramps just naturally go together. It is our favorite family outing since the women and children can partake of this sport also.

For some reason, Mike usually has less luck with catching fish than the other boys, and gets some good-natured ribbing. Last year the boys caught trout all around him, and he hadn't caught a thing. About the fourth day, he was fishing beside Matthew and hooked a big one. "Oh, boy," he gasped. "I've finally got one!" He fought it around for a while and finally landed it. It was a large, horny-headed chub. He told Matthew viciously, "If you tell this, I'll kill you!"

The boys went squirrel hunting last week, and their father went also. He stuck a handful of .20-gauge shotgun shells in his pocket, and strolled happily through the woods.

After he had killed a couple of the furry creatures, he started ejecting the shells out of his gun. One wouldn't come out, and when he investigated, he found that he had inserted a Chap Stick in his gun along with his ammunition.

⋯⟩═◑═⟨⋯

Bob, Patty's new husband, purchased a safety harness to use with his tree stand. When Patty asked him if he needed help in putting it on, he replied tersely that he had to learn to put it on himself. A little chastened, she sat down on the couch and began looking at a magazine.

He huffed and puffed, struggled and wallowed, until he finally succeeded in getting the thing across his back. "How do I look?" he asked Patty proudly. She could barely answer for laughing. She said he looked like Tarzan who had swung into a particularly tangled web of grape vines.

You could have helped me," he said in a hurt tone. "Well, excuse me!" she replied. "I thought you said you wanted to learn to do it yourself!"

⋯⟩═◑═⟨⋯

Criss constructed himself a "hunting shanty" that is unique. He put it together in front of the garage, and endured some good-natured ribbing. One daughter-in-law asked, "What are you building, a johnny house? It needs a quarter moon cut in the door!" Then one suggested that it looked like a bus house, except it had a door. It also had a neat little window and a window seat.

Bekah and Savannah, two of the great-grands, used it for a playhouse. One of the sons yelled, "I know what it is!

It's a 'poutin' house' for Dad to use when Mom throws him out of the house and he has no place to sleep!"

Criss just grinned sort of smugly and retorted, "Just wait until you all are up in your tree stands and the snow is blowing and the cold wind is freezing your hind legs off—I'll be sung and warm in my little deer house!" Yes, he'll be snug and warm all right—and probably fast asleep.

We have had some hilarious things happen during hunting season. But one of the funniest involved my nephew Eric and his beagle, Buster. As all good dogs eventually do, Buster grew old and was no longer able to chase the way he use to.

One day Eric saw a rabbit run through the yard, and he tried to get Buster's attention. Evidently, Buster had lost his sense of smell as well as his eyesight, for he couldn't detect the rabbit. Eric grew frustrated and grabbed up Buster in his arms and began chasing the rabbit. I don't think they caught it.

This must be a snaky time of year. Some of the young people were painting the church basement and discovered a litter of baby blacksnakes. It reminded me of the time that we had some hatch out in the washhouse, where we also had a shower stall. We had caught a glimpse of them a time or two, and one night I heard Criss yelling as he went to take a shower. I rushed in to find him beating the tar out of a black shoestring. Yes, he has since gotten eyeglasses.

One of our good friends, "Dood" Walker and his co-worker Rick Green accidentally ran over a fluffy white cat and killed it. Dood is such a good, conscientious boy that he was heartsick over it. He knocked at nearby houses, trying to find the owner, to no avail. They decided to bury it; it was the least that they could do. It was a steaming hot day, and the ground was hard and dry. Rick looked up from his labors, wiping the sweat from his brow and said, "Goodness, Dood, I hope you don't hit a cow tomorrow!"

Matthew finally got a turkey. After futile days of stalking a wild one, he gave up and bought a tame Tom turkey. He turned him loose with my chickens, and he promptly flew up on the chicken house roof, spread his wings, and took to the woods. Matthew caught him, put him in the lot again, and he repeated his performance. I then named him "Goodbye, Ten Bucks."

The turkey kept ranging farther and farther into the woods, so Matthew decided to capture him and shut him up inside the chicken house. He was impossible to lure in, so Matthew tracked him down and found him roosting on the limb of a tree. He borrowed a bucksaw and sawed the limb off, the turkey fell on top of him, and he nabbed him. He's trying to find some turkey eggs today. I didn't have the heart to tell him that old tom turkey will never set on those eggs. Things are never dull around the farm.

Patty caught a bright green June bug the other day, and tied a string to one of its legs. (We used to have so much fun doing that!) Her boys were enchanted, and played with the buzzing insect for hours. A couple of days later, Luke ran in the house just bubbling. "Mommy, you 'member that bug we played with the other day?" he asked. "Oh, that June bug?" she answered. "Yeah," he replied softly. "I just found a tiny, new-borned one." Tenderly cupped in his grubby, little hands was a Japanese beetle.

Life here can be peaceful and serene. I sat on the back porch last night and watched the lightning bugs rise up from the grass, sparkling in the velvet darkness and floating upward to meet the twinkling of the stars far above them. The deep thrum of a bullfrog vibrated through the stillness, and the plaintive cry of a whippoorwill sounded nearby. I could feel God's presence, so near and comforting. My life here in the hills is indeed blessed.

The funniest rabbit tale I ever heard happened years ago when my brother Larry was a kid at home. He was rabbit hunting with Dennie Payne, a neighbor boy. Dennie's family owned a first class rabbit beagle. The dog ran a rabbit in a drainpipe, and they couldn't get it out. The beagle grew frantic, running from one end of the pipe to the other, barking furiously.

Dennie's father came to help them, and he sent Dennie to the house for a pint of gasoline. He poured the gasoline in one end of the pipe and struck a match to it. There was a loud "whoom" and the pipe flew up six or more inches in the air, and then settled back down. Just then a naked rabbit, with all the hair singed from it, shot through the pipe and ran down over the hill.

The beagle took one startled look at it, tucked his tail between his legs and hid under the house; where no amount of persuasion could lure him back out. I'm afraid an experience like that would finish Clyde completely.

The fishermen in our family are looking forward to fishing season, although some diehards fish right through the snow and sleet. Trout season has officially opened on Williams River, as Cousin Don went up early in February and took his annual plunge into the icy water. He falls in every year, so we know then that the season has begun.

I guess Matthew didn't want to be outdone, so he made an excursion up there a few weeks later and fell in headlong. It was one of those cold, windy days when fishing lines dipped in the water came out frozen stiff, and Matthew was immediately chilled to the bone.

He came back to the truck, shucked off his waders, and turned the heater on full blast. He changed into dry clothes and went back to the river. He fell in again.

Country Food

Dieting and women seem to go together. I hope that you all are having better luck than I am. I've been laboring under a delusion all these years. I've always had the idea that diet soda would counteract a dozen chocolate chip cookies—and that cookie dough is less fattening than the finished product. When the plate of warm cookies is passed around, I say primly, "No, thank you; I'm on a diet." I don't tell them that I ate a pint of the cookie dough while I was baking them.

Cookie dough is good. When Kevin was a little boy, he loved cookie dough. "When I get married," he would say, "I'm going to mix up a whole bowl of cookie dough and eat it all myself!" (My boys never said, "When I grow up, or "when I leave home." I guess to them getting married was a mark of adulthood.) I don't know if Kevin ever ate a bowl of cookie dough or not. He looks as if he did.

My cousin Garrett (we called him Jeep then) asked Aunt Addie to make him some cookies. She mixed up a bowl of soft, sweet dough, and he asked her if he could eat some of it. Being the sort of aunt that she was, of course she said yes. He crammed several wads of dough in his mouth while she baked the first batch.

When the first ones came out of the oven, hot and tasty, he tried a baked one. Then he announced grandly, "I'll just eat these—you can throw the rest of that dough away!"

Food experts shy away from diets, and emphasize the theory of learning a new life style of eating habits to stick with the rest of your life. I pine for the good old days when fat grams were unheard of. We would come to the house, after a full morning of sledding, snowball fighting, and wallowing in the snow. We would be famished. A kettle of Mom's homemade potato soup would be simmering on the stove, and the mouth-watering aroma of onions and garlic would waft past our noses.

It was a robust soup, full of fresh whole milk and cream, liberally laced with real cow butter. We ate it with big, hot biscuits bountifully spread with more butter. No one would have recognized a fat gram if it slid off his chin.

We all had evening chores to do, and were starving when the supper meal was ready. We made short work of the huge bowls of fresh pork ribs, potatoes fried in bacon grease, and always hot biscuits or cornbread. Sometimes Mom would fix a pot of chicken and dumplings from the flock of chickens we kept.

There are no chicken dumplings to compare with those made from a "homemade" chicken. Yellow and tender, swimming in rich yellow chicken broth, it is food fit for a king. She would cook brown beans with great hunks of cured pork skin, which we loved to fish out and eat with vinegar or mustard. Yet we never had a weight problem.

Do you remember "soakies?" Mom said that she ate them when she was just a little girl. Criss' mother was the first person I saw make it. She would take a hot biscuit, butter it well, and drop it in a cup of hot coffee that had been well creamed. Then she ate it with a spoon. She must have fed her sons gallons of it.

Mom would never let us have coffee while we were growing up, as she said it would stunt our growth. The only time we were allowed to have it was when we were on a camping trip. Then we would lean back and feel so grown up, pretending to enjoy it, while in reality we could hardly stand the bitter brew.

My boys loved Grandma's soakies. If it stunted their growth, I can't tell it. They are all strapping six-footers, except poor Mike. He must have inherited my short, fat genes.

Eating habits have changed through the years, but I'll never forget one particular sandwich that my brother Mark witnessed. He was working on a construction job in another area, when lunchtime came and the men sat down and opened their lunch kits. One man produced a sandwich from his bucket and took the top slice of bread off to reveal the contents. It was a boiled pig ear, white and rubbery.

One man stood up, dropped his half-eaten sandwich in

the garbage can and walked away. Mark laughed. You can't help being impressed by a pig ear sandwich though.

My friend Hollis was telling me of the many people that his mother fed on Sunday when he was a boy. They attended church services in an old school house, and various itinerant preachers came in and held preaching services from time to time. His mother prided herself in being a good cook, and she considered it her duty to invite the visiting preacher and his friends to Sunday dinner.

There were 12 children in his family, and they had to wait in the shadows and starve while the adults and the preacher's assemblage stuffed themselves. One Sunday, those who were honored to eat at the first table gathered around a groaning board heaped with platters of fried chicken, bowls of garden vegetables, preserves and relishes, and an assortment of desserts.

She had made a pone of hot corn bread, cut it in squares, and piled it on a plate. The visiting preacher took one horrified look at the bread and announced in loud and ringing tones, "Sister, we can't eat here! You have cut the bread, and the Bible plainly states that we are to break bread. It's a sin to cut bread!"

Gathering up his probably reluctant entourage, they all stalked out of the house. Hollis' mother, who had worked long and hard over a hot stove, was shocked and humiliated, and of course in tears. Not so the children—Hollis said it was the one time they got all the fried chicken they could eat. "In fact," he said gleefully, "I had a notion to slip around after each service and tell the preacher that Mom didn't break the bread—she cut it!"

We are blessed here in the hills, with the abundance of wild foods that are ours for the gathering. Wild nuts are plentiful, although the walnuts are sort of messy to hull. After the hull softens, usually by frost, they are easier to do. We used to jack up the rear wheel of the family car, and pour the unhulled walnuts under the tire. The tire would spin around and mash the hulls off efficiently.

Hickory nuts are tedious to crack, but the flavor is so exquisite that it is worth the effort. We always look for the shellbark hickory trees, as the shell is thinner and the nutmeats bigger.

Our ancestors found many uses for the wild nuts that were growing here in such abundance. The husks of the black walnut provided a blackish dye used for their clothing, while the butternut bark yielded a orange or yellow color. The inner bark of the hickory was used to make a yellow dye.

Although we no longer have to dye material for the clothes we wear (or sew the garment either) we still gather the wild nuts and use them in our cooking. We gather wild greens, mushrooms, and the men folk bring in wild game. What can be better than the wild foods we use when we camp out and fish? The hillsides yield ramps, the river trout. We feast on potatoes fried over an open campfire, lovely tender ramps cooked with eggs, and pan-fried trout. It doesn't get any better than that.

Thanksgiving brought hog butchering time and our supply of meat for the winter. Sausage, ribs and backbones, and sometimes the shoulders were canned, lard was rendered, and the hams and sides of bacon were smoked. The skin of the hog was rendered in the oven for additional lard, and we used the crisp cracklings in corn bread. We also ate the crunchy pork rinds.

The feet were scraped and pickled. The head was cooked in a huge pot, and the meat picked off to make souse, or head cheese. The ears were cooked and added to it. We used almost everything about the hog, except his grunt. We ate the heart and liver, but we didn't eat the lungs.

One old-timer, who lived high up on the mountain here years ago, had a sick spell right after hog-killing time. His wife told my dad that Bill had eaten a "whole set of hog lights."

Mom did use all the extra scraps of fat to make homemade soap. We used it for laundry, scrubbing, and general cleaning. Her soap was white and clean smelling, and the girls in the family declare that it is a better stain remover than anything they can buy. When used as a shampoo, it is a sure cure for dandruff.

We utilize a lot of wild game. Criss has made rabbit sausage, which is leaner than pork sausage. It does need a chunk of fresh pork ground up with it, as it is too lean to fry. He cuts the rabbit off the bone, combines it with ground pork, sage, salt, brown sugar, and sage or sausage seasoning. It makes a tasty, lean sausage.

I have a recipe in my Louisiana cookbook, which I have never tried. It's for "Possum Sausage" and some adventuresome soul may want to try it. First, you catch and kill eight or ten 'possums during the wintertime. Hang them out until frost hits them. (?) Skin and cut all the meat from the bone. Grind 'possum meat, adding salt, sage, dried and ground red pepper, and black pepper to taste. Smoke and place meat in sack; leave in smokehouse until ready to eat.

One of my good friends gave me a recipe for Baked 'Possum that I haven't tried. You start with one 'possum—no roadkill please!

Skin, dress and scald in boiling water. Rub inside and out with salt and pepper. Make a stuffing with breadcrumbs, applesauce, and sliced chestnuts. (There were no exact measurements given—I guess you have to adjust the amount to the size of your 'possum.)

Fill 'possum with stuffing mix, place in roaster, and cover with sliced sweet potatoes. Add one cup of water, ½ cup lemon juice, and ¾ cup of butter. Baste often, cook until tender, and don't call me when it is done.

December is here, and the holiday season looms closer. Area cooks are digging out their favorite recipes to begin baking the seasonal treats that we all love. I'll never forget the coconut candy that my Aunt Addie made one year.

She had a fresh coconut that was just slightly past its prime, so she decided to shred it and make some candy. It turned out perfect, so her son Bill took some to his teacher, Mrs. Wolfe. "This is delicious, Billy." She exclaimed. "How did your mother make it?" Bill solemnly replied, "Well, first, you take a rotten coconut . . . "

Mom went up to spend the night with Susie, and took her a pound of bacon and a freshly-baked apple pie. Ronnie absent-mindedly set the box down beside the truck and forgot to take it in. The next morning there was an empty pie pan and some chewed paper off the bacon.

Noel, who was unaware of what happened, paraded his dog by and asked, "Don't you think my dog is looking better?" Mom said grimly, "He ought to—he just had a pound of Oscar Meyer bacon and a whole apple pie!" I guess he had a happy Thanksgiving, too.

The boys brought back a huge sack of ramps and decided to clean and cook them. I had gone to a baby shower, and when I returned, I could actually smell them out in the driveway with the doors and windows closed in the house. Kevin sighed with satisfaction. "Doesn't the house smell good? It smells just like a fishing trip!" (He was serious.) Yes, it smelled all right—like King Tut's tomb when it was first opened to the light of day.

I know now how my youngest sister Susie felt when we

all ate ramps on a fishing trip except her. There were about fifteen of us crowded into one big tent, and she suffered. "Breathe some other way," she would beg. "And please don't laugh!" I believe that the family that eats ramps together will always stay together. No one else would have us.

We take advantage of the wild food around us. We eat what is killed, or give some to neighbors who are unable to hunt. It's been a good squirrel season; in fact, Criss has overloaded me with them. It seems that every evening there is a sink full of raw squirrels for me to package and freeze. I began to complain a little mildly, asking him if he couldn't slack up on the squirrels, or else hunt and not kill any.

He was highly indignant. "Put them in the freezer," he retorted. "We'll eat them." I had to carry it further. "But we are getting too many!" I complained. In exasperation he informed me, "I'll bring them home; you just cook them." So I decided I would.

On Wednesday evening we had fried squirrel, which was delicious; on Thursday, we had squirrel and gravy, with sweet potatoes. Friday's menu was the same, with squirrel and gravy. Saturday evening he came in, cold and hungry. "What's for supper?" he inquired eagerly. "Squirrel," I answered sweetly. He looked dumbfounded. "Again?" he questioned, less eagerly. "I thought you liked squirrel," I told him innocently. "Well, I do," he said slowly. "But I ain't a plumb fool about it!"

A friend of my sister's family, a young man named Tom, was out in the woods recently. He was feeling close to nature, and very peaceful, as he dug up and ate the roots of a plant that we call "Adam and Eve." At least, he thought that was what it was. He could feel vitality run through his veins as nature's herbs supplied nutrients to his body.

It soon became apparent that it was not "Adam and Eve" he was chewing, but Indian turnip. He was about a mile from the house, and no water anywhere. He was so desperate that he stuffed his mouth full of dirt, and ran home. It was a startled wife to say the least, when she opened the door to a wild-eyed husband, rivulets of dirt running down his chin, and mumbling incoherently.

When he fastened his mouth over the kitchen faucet, she realized it was water he was croaking for. I guess the moral of the story is be careful, or the Indians will still have their revenge.

My cousin Phyllis dearly loves grouse. It is the only wild meat she is truly fond of, and her brothers try to get her one each season. Grouse season had almost passed, and they had no bird to offer her. Don had a bright idea, and shared his plan with his younger brother, Tony. It seems that Don had a banty rooster there on the farm, a feisty little fellow that would fight a circle saw. Everyone walked a wide path around him, including the big rooster that guarded the laying hens.

He was not wet behind the ears, either. Don wasn't sure of his age, but he must have been in the senior citizen bracket. His spurs had grown out so long that he had to walk bow-legged to keep from catching together and throwing him. Don sneaked up on him and caught him, and then fastened him in a box in the back of Tony's truck.

Unsuspecting, Tony lifted the lid to see what was in the box, to be greeted with a flurry of wings, sharp beak, and furious, beady eyes. For a minute he could have sworn it had 12 rattles and a button but then he realized it was the banty rooster. He was glad to dispatch it.

He dressed it carefully, and carried it to his sister Phyllis with love. She received the "grouse" with heartfelt gratitude, and promptly set about making Tony a lovely batch of homemade fudge.

The next day she decided to cook her grouse. She boiled it for two hours and then baked it for two hours. She remarked to her husband, "Darrell, this is the toughest grouse I ever tried to cook!"

In the meantime, Tony's conscience had smote him sorely. With each piece of fudge, he felt worse. "Don." He asked his brother, "How many times does the Bible say you must forgive?" "Oh, about 490 times," Don replied. Tony pondered, "Well, do you think Phyllis will forgive me one time for the trick we played on her?"

With his courage in hand, he made his way back to his sister's house. Fate intervened, as it so often does, before he arrived. A neighbor stopped him and asked, "Tony, do you want this grouse? I shot it this morning." With a thankful heart, Tony accepted the grouse. Phyllis finally got her bird, and Tony got his fudge and a clear conscience.

Phyllis had the last laugh, however. She cooked the rooster again the next day, and said it was better than any

grouse she ever ate. The moral in this story is quite clear—
a bird in the hand may not be the same one in the bush.

Back in the "good old days" I spent a lot of time with my
friend, Peggy Ann. We slept under half a dozen handmade
quilts in the upstairs of their big old house on the hill, and
it was some of the best times of our youth. One night Reva
Jeanine and I were both staying the night, and the next
morning Peggy's mother Beulah made "chocolate syrup"
and biscuits.

Beulah was fretting about her biscuits that just hadn't
turned out "right." "I don't know what is the matter with the
biscuits this morning," she fussed. "They didn't raise at all."
Reva looked up and said sweetly, "They tried," Aunt Beulah.
"They squatted."

Our eating habits and customs have changed drastically
since I was a child. Children were seen, not heard, and
sometimes it felt as if we weren't seen much either. When
we had company for a meal, and the table was crowded, we
sat quietly until the guests and adults had eaten and left
the table. Then it was our turn.

Mom came from a family of 11 children, and sometimes
when they had guests it would be the third table before she
got to eat. By that time, the chicken neck and a few scraps
were about all that were left. Now we feed the children first
and get them out of the way so we can enjoy our meal in
peace.

◆⟶◎⟻◆

The old-timey customs still prevail here, as they do in most small communities in the mountains. Folks don't have to be invited to visit; they just drop in. If it is mealtime, they will be invited to join the family. (Wouldn't this surprise a city dweller?)

Grandpa and Grandma O'Dell were known for their hospitality. They were real "clever" folks. Scarcely a meal passed that someone didn't join them at their table. I remember Grandpa telling about a neighbor lady who always "just happened" to drop in at supper time every evening.

They would invite her to eat, and she would run to the door and yell to her husband, "Ho, Har'son (Harrison) if'n yore a'wantin' anything to eat, you'd better be gottin' yourself on down here!" Har'son would be hiding in the woods until the call came.

◆⟶◎⟻◆

We love wilted lettuce, which is fresh garden lettuce fixed with hot bacon grease-vinegar dressing. We'd never heard it called "killed" lettuce until we had guests from North Carolina. Crystal says that is what her in-laws (originally from Kentucky) call it.

The first time she ate at their home, her mother-in-law served a delicious-looking bowl of fresh lettuce. Crystal told her how well she liked it, and she pressed a huge serving on her. Crystal took one eager bite, and realized the only dressing on it was bacon grease. As soon as her mother-in-law disappeared in the kitchen, she hurriedly told her husband Jeff, "Take this quick—I can't eat it!"

He hastily scooped it on his plate, just as his mother returned. "Why, Crystal," she exclaimed, "You've already eaten all your lettuce! Here, have some more." And she gave her another big serving. Crystal suddenly found herself so full that she couldn't possibly eat another bite.

The grandchildren and great-grands are good to help with the farm chores. Tammy and I picked two five-gallon buckets of green beans, and her three little girls helped. She took the beans home to can, and the girls plunged right in and began stringing them.

Rachel and Judy had been planning to raise their own garden next year and had discussed it endlessly. As they finished stringing the last of the beans, a tired Judy turned to Rachel and stated emphatically, "I'll tell you one thing, Rachel—when I raise my garden, I'm not going to grow any beans!"

Our son Andy has his garden right beside ours, and grandson Nicholas, who just turned three, is extremely proud of "his" garden. We were walking up the path beside the gardens, and he swung his arm expansively and announced, "Boy, MY broccoli is looking good! "Boy, MY green beans are too!"

He loves to argue with his grandpa about the ownership of the gardens. He and Criss were looking the crops over a few days ago, and Nicholas was in a generous mood. "Poppaw," he said, "You're a man, and I'm a boy-man. We'll just share this garden!"

My baby sister Susie once made a cake for a boyfriend who was coming to call that afternoon. She stirred, baked, and turned the finished product out on a platter. It broke open like Mt. Vesuvius. She filled it full of frosting, and then it looked like Crater Lake. Disgusted, she took the whole mess out and dumped it under a rock cliff behind our house.

She was living with us at the time, and while she and her boyfriend were chatting, I dug out the cake and brought it in to show him what a good cook Susie was. She felt like smothering me to death in the frosting. The romance didn't get off the ground, but I don't think it was because of the cake—I hope. She should have smothered me in the icing.

Family Feud

One of my young neighbors, who is quite near-sighted, has a phobia about the dark. As a consequence, she leaves a night-light burning in her hall, another in the bathroom, and a third in her bedroom. She also sleeps in her eyeglasses because she can't bear to wake up and not be able to see.

The electricity went off in the night a while back, and she woke up in total darkness. Timidly, she turned on the light switch—it was still completely dark. "Oh, Edward," she said softly, "I've gone blind!"

A dear friend of mine described her husband as a good person and father, but he doesn't know how to do anything around the house. She had a water pipe burst in her house one time, and while the water was swirling ankle deep around her, she was frantically sweeping it. Just then her husband stepped in. "Help me, Ed," she screamed. "Do something!" So he took the broom from her and started sweeping.

We love our neighbors, but sometimes they are funny. One of our neighbors, an older man, was walking up the road one time when he looked over in a yard and saw a couple fighting. It was a brother and sister who lived together, and they were really fisting it out. As he finished his errand and was walking back down the road, he met the lady.

"Did you get hurt in the fracas?" he asked her. She replied shortly, "No—I got hurt right above the fracas!"

One of our good neighbors had lived a long and fruitful life, and was nearing the end. She was in the hospital, and took a turn for the worse. They called her children and kinfolk in, and in a short time, she got better. She apologized to them for making a trip to the hospital, and then added, "But didn't we have a good turn out?"

Patty met one of our neighbors in the grocery store a few days back, and the lady had lost a good bit of weight. Patty complimented her, and asked "How in the world did you lose that much?" The lady answered airily, "Oh, I just kept eatin' them Roman numerals!" (Ramen noodles)

One of the funniest blunders happened years ago while Criss was still working. Gerald was his loyal helper and sidekick, and they were paving at the Capitol complex. They stopped to eat their lunch just as the state house workers came streaming out of the building.

Criss probably exaggerated the fact that Gerald was staring at a beautiful young woman when he stubbed his toe and fell splat on the sidewalk, breaking his metal dinner bucket in two pieces. It was probably just a tale that the young women looked curiously down at him as they passed. Poor Gerald! He never lived that down.

Lovel Everson, our lifelong neighbor who lived to the ripe old age of 94, was recalling the boom times when oil and gas was discovered here in Ovapa. He worked with many of the old timers, including Clay Bullard, Boone Strickland, Charlie Six, Oral Dye, Jim Yoak and many others. One of his best friends was Aaron Short, and he worked with him for years.

"One day Aaron come up to me," he reminisced, "and without warning began pouring the fist to me." Completely astonished, he asked, "What on earth is the matter with you, Aaron? Are you going crazy?" Between blows to my chest he explained, "Well, I'm about to get in a fight with my brother-in-law, Ray King. I figured if I could whip you, I could give him a licking!"

My cousin Don owned a grocery store and a lumber supply place, and one snowy morning he walked out the door to spy a couple of young men standing there with a large snow shovel. He asked the boys what they were up to, and they started telling him excitedly.

"Don," one of them spluttered, "We're gonna make a lot of money. We bought this snow shovel, and we're gonna shovel snow for people—and say, Don, why don't you let us shovel the snow from the front of your store?"

Don explained that he had several people on the payroll and he had someone to shovel his snow. The boys were not so easily deterred though, and began again. "Aw, c'mon, Don, let us shovel your parking lot, we'll do you a good job, we won't charge you very much; you can afford it, huh, Don?" Don explained again that he was paying men to do that sort of thing, and he didn't need them.

Still the boys persevered, "Aw, Don, just let me shovel a path from the grocery store to the building supply store. We'll only charge you a couple of dollars, okay?" Don said firmly, "Look, boys, I told you I don't need you to do my shoveling!"

The boys were silent for a minute, then one of them said, "Well, shoot, how much will you give us for this snow shovel?"

⊷⟾◉⟾⊷

Mary Ellen's youngest son David was watching his grandpa do some mowing, when Poppy stopped to sharpen his scythe. He laid his whetstone on a nearby rock and admonished David, "Now don't you bother that—it's real easy to break." David calmly picked up the whetstone and whacked it across the rock. "Look here, Poppy," he said. "Now you've got two." Dad had to laugh.

⊷⟾◉⟾⊷

Aunt Ruby used to send her two sons, Garrett and Neal, up to our house to help hoe out the field corn. "Now you're not to pay them," admonished Aunt Ruby. "This is just an accommodation." Mom was milking two cows at the time, and gave their family sweet milk. After all the "accommodation" she would still try to pay Mom for the milk, and the children would try to press payment upon her. Mom was just as adamant in refusing payment.

One day my youngest brother, Ronnie (always the black sheep) waited until the cousins started walking back down the road. He was out of earshot of Mom, and chased them down. He gasped, "Mom changed her mind—she wants the money." A little startled, they nevertheless turned the change over to Ronnie.

Ronnie promptly lit out for Opal's General Store, where he squandered his ill-gotten gains on candy and pop. In due time the foul deed was discovered, and of course he had to pay the piper.

I'll never forget the time when he was a teenager and went fishing. He caught an eighteen-wheeler. He was down on Laurel Creek along Route 4, and cast his line out just as the big truck came whizzing by. The hook caught on the truck, his line went "whirr" and Ronnie was left with an empty reel and a silly look on his face.

The road to true love, or otherwise, is many times fraught with stumbling blocks. My late Uncle Enos used to tell the sad saga of one of his young friends named Odie. He was sweet on a certain girl, but like John Alden, he was too bashful to do his own courting. He bought her a box of candy and prevailed upon Uncle Enos and his friend Elmer to give it to her.

He should have known better—Uncle Enos was quite a jokester, and it was like asking a fox to guard the chicken house. He and Elmer ate the whole bottom layer of candy, and replaced it with tiny potatoes re-wrapped in the gold foil.

Odie was hurt and perplexed when he saw the girl later and she refused to speak to him. I wonder if the whole course of history was changed for him by Uncle Enos' Valentine prank. Puppy love is sweet, if it doesn't go to the dogs.

The Seamy Side of Life

As I cleaned out the chicken house this week, I thought that this is one aspect of our memories that are sometimes forgotten as we reminisce: the seamier side of country living. We mention the old johnny house with a sly grin, but we had to clean out barns and chicken houses too—and scatter the natural fertilizer on the garden. Everything about the farm wasn't necessarily roses.

It was one of my summertime jobs to go after the cows in the evening and bring them back to the barn to be milked. I would walk behind them, daydreaming, until the soft splat, splat, splat in front of me and my bare feet stepping in the warm stuff brought me back to earth.

Mom and my granddaughter, Chrissie, were out in the pasture field a few days ago hunting paw paws. Chrissie has spent her tender years in the state of Louisiana, and farm living is new to her. "Mom-Granny, what is this soft stuff I'm walking through?" she asked Mom. She was more interested than revolted when Mom explained to her about cow patties and the facts of life.

I've been thinking about the little brown shack out back. In our case, it was more of a weather-beaten gray. I told Mom that I missed the old toilet, and she looked at me like I was crazy. Well, I have a lot of fond memories of that place. You can call it a closet, as Mom's family did when she was a child. Grandpa O'Dell called it a "backhouse" but we mostly called it the johnny house. But whatever you called it, it was a mighty important place. (A rose by any other name would smell as sweet?)

I spent a lot of my growing-up days in that building. It was not a physical problem by any means, but I loved to read. I kept a book hid in the overlapping tin on the roof, and made plenty of trips to that little gray shack when I should have been doing my chores.

Our modern bathrooms just don't have the same atmosphere that the old-time privies had. While I sat and read and dreamed, I could hear the lazy humming of the bees outside, the clear melody of a songbird, or the melodic tinkle of a cowbell up in the pasture field. And it seemed that you weren't disturbed half so much then.

Before I get two paragraphs read now in the bathroom, someone is pounding on the door demanding their turn. (Probably Crystal, wanting to read too.) I will admit that it wasn't too much fun to get an attack of the "whoopie-doopies" at midnight on a cold winter night, and have to beg someone to go with you because you were afraid. Poor Mary Ellen would always take pity on me and go along.

When my nephew Douglas was a little boy, his daddy Larry got him a skin-diving outfit consisting of flippers, a facemask, and a snorkel tube. He donned the complete outfit, and wandered into the bathroom where his older sister (one of the twins) was perched on the necessary seat.

"Could you direct me to the nearest ocean?" he mumbled through his facemask. By the time she got through thumping his head, he was looking for directions to the nearest first-aid station. Now that would never have happened in the outdoor johnny house. I have fond memories of that place.

Mirror Mirror

I remember a few years back that I tried making sauerkraut in a food processor. It made such a mushy product that I didn't try it again. On that day, however, I had moved the food processor to the back porch to eliminate the mess in the kitchen, and was grinding away. I was standing barefoot on the ground, with chopped cabbage draped liberally on my elbows, feet and dress. I sensed someone standing beside me, and my eyes traveled to his snow-white tennis shoes, up his sharply creased slacks to his neat sport shirt, and settled on his amused face. It was Reuel Foote, one of Criss' old school buddies that we hadn't seen for many years. That seems to be the story of my life.

It was almost that bad a few weeks ago when Bicycle Bill Curry brought his mother up to meet me. I was at daughter Patty's attending a grandchild's birthday party, and had just eaten a bowl of Superman ice cream. In case you are not acquainted with this kid's treat, it is a violent blue color, along with neon yellow. It also stains your teeth and mouth bright blue, which doesn't wash off for some time. My hair was falling down, and I'd just added another hair net, which was drooping down my back. (It could have been because I'd just been dumped out of a hammock on my head.) They were friendly and gracious, and pretended not to notice. Sometimes I feel as if I am blowing my image.

I have been trying hard to improve my image, and I want you to know that it is a real battle. I sadly fear that these excursions into the woods and fields don't help much. Our family reunion is coming up in less than a month, and it is my desire to look svelte, cultured, and well groomed. I went on a diet, and so far I have gained two pounds. No matter how hard I try, my clothes usually look like Chrissy's after she has climbed an apple tree and descended on her head.

I can slick my hair back and glue it down. But before I get to my destination it looks somewhat like a softball with a split cover and the innards raveling out. I also manage to create a terrible first impression.

One day last week, I allowed myself the luxury of sleeping late. Honestly, it was the first morning in ages that I hadn't gotten up at 5:30 or 6:00 and stayed up. I donned an old housecoat that Goodwill had rejected years ago, and on my feet were a pair of misshapen house shoes that had died three months before and I hadn't gotten around to burying yet.

I had just brushed out my hair preparing to shampoo it when there came a sudden knock on the door. Hastily wadding up my hair in a lopsided granny knot, I answered the door. There stood a strange gentleman. He explained that he had read my column for some time and had expressed a desire to meet me.

After chatting for a while, he said lamely, "You don't look like I thought you'd look!" Well—I don't look like I thought I'd look, either. Sometimes I get shock when I get a glimpse of myself in a mirror. Usually, I try not to look.

Still, I am trying. One rainy day a few days ago, I went to the chicken house to gather the eggs. I couldn't carry an umbrella and the eggs too, so I pulled a plastic shower cap over my head to protect my hairdo. Just as I stepped out of the chicken house, my hands full of eggs, one of my husband's friends drove up beside me and stopped.

I simply pretended that my chapeau was straight from Paris, and chatted quite pleasantly with him. I could feel him eyeing my polka-dotted headgear a little strangely as he drove off.

I don't know why I expect to suddenly grow more graceful in my mature years when I wasn't that way when I was younger. I try; I really do. I meet real ladies who trip forward gracefully on slender high heels to shake my hand, while my feet get tangled up in my sensible low-heeled loafers.

They smile charmingly and converse in well-modulated tones about current events and interesting places they have been. I grin widely and apologize to them for being late, and explain how the hogs got out at the last minute and how I fell out the chicken house door in the mud after I was ready to leave.

They can still smile gracefully as they back away saying they would really like to stay and chat, but they are dreadfully late for an appointment.

It's hopeless, I know. Many years ago, when I was much younger and tried harder to be a lady, an incident happened that brought me back to earth. I was in a doctor's office and met a handsome gentleman who struck up an interesting conversation with me.

I was wearing an undergarment known as a waist-pincher, which was equipped with plastic "bones" to nip in the waistline. We finished our conversation, and I got up to make my exit. Just as I passed in front of him, one of the bones slid out of my girdle and fell in the floor. I never looked back.

Some people can even commit a faux pas gracefully. My sister Jeannie has a sister-in-law who is elegant in dress, manner and speech. Jeannie admits that she feels like a klutz around her. This summer they were visiting Betty in Charlotte and planned a family picnic and outing.

Betty worked all morning on a fancy punch bowl cake (she is also a superb cook) made with angel food cake, strawberries and whipped cream. Attired all in white, from her snowy blouse and tailored slacks down to her white anklets and gleaming Nikes, she stepped lightly down the path to the picnic table, proudly bearing her splendid creation.

All at once she caught her toe on a rock and tripped headlong, plunging her face square into the punch bowl full of cake. She hung onto the bowl for dear life, and arose dripping with strawberries and whipped cream. Carefully carrying the mutilated cake to the picnic table, she wiped her face with perfect aplomb and smilingly presented the cake to her guests.

We may have a mental image of how we look, but a glance in the mirror dispels that notion. Did you ever think of how our grandchildren see us? I found an essay written by Luke for his English class when he was in high school. I am not sure it is flattering, but it is enlightening.

From his beginning, Luke has been a surprise to me. (He is special, just as all of my grandchildren are.) The first surprise was that he was a boy. After five grandsons, I was more than ready to welcome a baby girl in the family. This was the days before ultrasound tests took out most of the guesswork and almost all the excitement. To me, it's sort of like peeking into your Christmas gift before the big day.

When his father came into the waiting room to announce, "We've got another boy!" I was totally flabbergasted. I had myself firmly convinced that he was a girl. He has been surprising us ever since.

Luke always went his own way; marching to a drum beat only he could hear. He never talked until he was almost three, relying on his older brother Aaron to interpret his grunts and pointed finger. When they played "cowboys and Indians," Aaron even had to make the bang-bang sound for Luke's gun.

One day his mother Patty and I were in the house and Luke was playing outside. He came through the door and calmly stated, "It's raining out there." Patty screeched, "He talked!" I guess he hadn't anything of importance to say until then.

We didn't know he could write, but then we didn't know he could talk either. Here is his essay:

"My grandmother is a short, elderly woman who always has a smile and a sparkle in her eye. Her brown hair, which is now almost all gray, seems to ride on her head like a small crown of silver. Just below her hairline, she has a pair of small, beady eyes that hide behind a pair of glasses that seem to hang onto her nose like a monkey to a tree.

"Her lips are small, thin and pink, but are always giving encouragement and advice to any number of her grandchildren. Her chin is always pointing in the direction she is going. Her shoulders, like those of the rest of her family, are broad and always laid back as if she is carrying all the pride of her family.

"My Mommaw, as we call her, is great when it comes to understanding, and many times makes her children listen to their kids before correcting them. As kids, me and my brothers always fought like cats and dogs. When Mom broke us up, I always ran to Mommaw for protection. Mommaw would always take up for me.

"One day in early July, my older brother and I were playing in the creek making a dam when I accidentally knocked a rock off it, and that was all it took to start a war of words that quickly turned into a fury of fists. My mom, who was in the garden not ten yards away, came running. Mommaw, who was coming down the road to have dinner with us, was not too far behind.

"After pulling us from the creek, Mom was ready to beat our bottoms, but was stopped by Mommaw, who insisted on hearing what had happened. After hearing Aaron's excuse about my trying to flood his toads, which just happened to slip away during the fight, Mom's fury quickly turned to laughter.

"After being rushed to the house by Mommaw to get cleaned up for dinner; I heard her tell Mommy, 'Kids are always going to have misunderstandings, and sometimes things just need to be worked out.' They didn't see me standing by the stove until I added, 'And if you keep picking switches, you'll kill all the trees!'

"Mommaw is also very loving, and she will stop what she is doing to play with us kids. One day my younger brother was staying with Mommaw, and he found a large box and attacked it with a hacksaw. He fashioned a post office, or at least that's what he called it. Later he claimed all the morning's junk mail, and raided the wastebasket for yesterday's discards.

"Mommaw claimed, as she drew a picture of the flag and printed the words 'Post Office' on one side of the box, 'Any grandmother worth her salt can find time to draw flags, write a few words, steam off a few stamps, and still find time to can beans.'

"Mommaw also has a great sense of humor that she expresses out loud. For example, late that day after my younger brother went home, she heard a knock on her back door. Opening it, she found Adrian standing there with his BB gun. He quickly asked, 'Mommaw, do you want to go hunting?'

"Her instant reply was, 'I wonder if a young kid and old grandma can bag some big game?' And as always, she flashed him a big grin and grabbed her coat."

At least I know how one grandchild sees me.

⊹⇒◐⇐⊹

One of these days I am going to compile a book on beauty

aids using natural ingredients, beginning with Crystal's famous dough treatment for hair. Our neighbor Kitty tried one out last week. She read a recipe for conditioning the hair, in which you blend a carrot until frothy and add it to your conditioner to make the hair soft and silky. She did. She spent the rest of the day picking tiny pieces of carrot out of her hair. I can't tell much difference in her hair, but she is seeing better at night.

While we were laughing at her, niece Kara confessed to a trick she used to curl her eyelashes. After she used the eyelash curler, she wanted something to make them stay curled. So—she sprayed them with hair spray. After she finally got her sight back, the curl was gone.

Jeannie told of the time that she couldn't find the Vaseline to use on her eyelashes, so she used Vick's salve. Need I say more?

If there is anyone qualified to write a book on style and beauty, it must be me. One day last week I was cleaning Crystal's room and I ran across a large blue silk flower which I stuck in the top of my hair. While I was running the sweeper, I couldn't hear a knock at my front door. Crystal came running upstairs to tell me that someone wanted me. I went to the door to find one of the high school teachers returning an item he had borrowed.

I conversed with him a little bit, but I noticed he looked

at me funny and left hurriedly. After he left I raised my hand up to my hair and felt that big blue flower sticking up like a solitary spotlight. "Oh, Crystal," I gasped, "Did I have that flower in my hair while Mike was here?"

"Yes, Mommy," she answered gleefully. "You also had it in your hair when the UPS man was here too!" I don't even want to know what they were thinking. Years ago, I longed to be young and beautiful. Then I settled for being (hopefully) older and interesting. Now I guess I'm just old and eccentric.

Spring-cleaning fever is beginning to affect me. I like to wait until it's warm enough to throw open all the doors and windows and thoroughly rout winter's dirt and grime. (What I'd really like to do is throw open the doors and march outside and stay.) There seems to be an inborn urge in most housewives to refurbish the old nest after the shut-up days of winter have taken their toll.

There is a class of housewives who religiously clean and rearrange their furniture at least once a week. I am not in that class. I move the furniture around about once a year, and the family gripes about that. My sister-in-law Alice once cleaned and rearranged her bedroom while Larry was at work.

He got off at midnight, and stumbled tiredly into the bedroom without turning on the lights. After undressing, he jumped thankfully into bed and fell flat in a bare corner of the bedroom. Alice had moved the bed to the other side of the room.

Cures For What Ails Ya

Warts seem to plague country kids (and probably their city counterparts as well) and there are almost as many "cures" as there are warts. Matthew's friend Kermit told him a sure cure. It seems that you steal a dishrag from your mother's kitchen, bury it secretly in the ground, and the wart will go away. Another remedy is to take the lining from a chicken's gizzard, rub it on your wart, and then bury it in the drip of the house.

My niece Julie says to take a piece of banana peeling, place it over the wart, tape a Band-Aid over it, and leave it until it rots. I don't know if she meant the wart rots, or the banana skin rots—maybe your arm. I've heard of rubbing a coin over the warts, and I think there is an incantation that goes along with it, but I don't know what it is.

My old mountain recipe book says that stump water is real good for warts and other skin ailments. Mom was familiar with this. She says to rub the stump water on the warts while reciting this chant, "Barley corn, barley corn, Injun meal, shorts/ Stump water, stump water/ Swaller these warts." The warts are supposed to disappear.

My Dad swore by mullein leaves for chest colds and coughs. These velvety leaves can be gathered any time of the year, so I waited impatiently for someone to come down with a cold so I could try them out. I gathered some of the fuzzy leaves and brewed a concoction according to my herb book.

This involved simmering the leaves in a pint of milk for ten minutes, then straining them through two layers of muslin cloth in order to remove the tiny hairs that would really irritate the throat. Sweetened with a tablespoon of honey, it was to be taken every few hours until it was gone. (Or maybe the cold or cough was gone.) I tasted a sip of it but it reminded me too much of the time I mixed sugar in my milk and Mom made me drink it for making a mess. Anyway, I wasn't sick, but Criss had a sore throat.

When I presented him with a sure cure for his throat, he shot me a suspicious look and demanded to know what was in it. When I told him, he flatly refused to taste one drop. I had to wait for the next victim, my daughter-in-law Sarah. She admitted to having congestion in her chest, but when I tried to cure her, she vowed she wouldn't touch that stuff with a ten foot pole. I don't know how they expect me to become a medicine woman if they won't let me "doctor" them.

I guess I shot my reputation as an herb doctor a long time ago. Andy came home from work with a severe bellyache, and I tried to doctor him with some fresh peppermint tea. He declined the offer, and went to a higher source—his grandmother. She insisted that we call the doctor. To make a long story short, he ended up in the hospital having emergency surgery for a "hot" appendix.

We do rely on yellow root (goldenseal) for sore throats and mouth sores. Made into a tea and gargled, it does work. It is as bitter as gall though, and there's not too much demand for it among the younger generation. I can always doctor myself though.

Winter is the best bark-gathering time, as medicinal barks are of the highest quality when gathered in the dormant season. The bark of the slippery elm, birch, wild cherry and the inner bark of the white pine can be gathered now. It is also time to gather the red berries of the sumac bush, to be used as an astringent and a gargle.

Wild ginger is blooming, its tiny, brown flower almost hidden in the crotch of its leafstalks. I like to nibble on the gingery-tasting root, although a little goes a long way. One of my herbal medicine books states that ginger root produces anti-inflammatory activity like that of the typical NSAID (non-steroidal anti-inflammatory drug) used for arthritis and other diseases.

It has recently received attention as an aid to prevent nausea and motion sickness. (Oh, how I wish I had known this when I was carrying my babies!) Ginger tea has long been used as a remedy for coughs and colds. Coltsfoot tea makes an effective cough syrup, and one can also make cough drops from it.

Along with wild herbs, I have always been interested in wild foods. We always used them when I was growing up; Mom would pick a dishpan full of mixed greens that she would cook for supper. We usually ate them with boiled potatoes, canned pork, and cornbread. That is still a delicious meal.

I've branched out a little farther now and tried some things that never occurred to Mom. My wild foods book recommended the common orange daylily as a good source of wild food. The unopened buds could be cooked as a vegetable, and the withered, mature flower could be used in soups.

I picked a quart or more of the firm buds, brought them home and prepared them. I washed my wild bounty and simmered them in some real butter with salt and pepper. They were delicious, tasting a bit like green beans. I must have eaten a pint of them, while Criss was more moderate and ate a small amount.

It wasn't long until I began feeling queasy, and soon after a bit nauseous. I wondered if I had picked up a 24-hour virus that was making its rounds. After I spent the rest of the evening alternating between the bed and the bathroom, I consulted my wild foods book. Sure enough, printed beneath the daylily recipes was this warning, "Try the buds sparingly at first; they may be cathartic." Life in the hills is not always a bed of orange daylilies.

While most mountain folk are familiar with wild greens, there are plenty of other wild foods waiting for an adventurous cook to try. Redbud "beans" give an oriental touch to stir fries, if gathered when they are new and tender. Lamb's quarter greens taste a lot like spinach, and are full of vitamins. Common purslane that grows in the garden in abundance is a substitute for okra. I have made a gumbo with it.

I am anxious to try catbrier shoots, but I'd better not

spring too many things on Criss at one time. I found a relative of the catbrier this morning, a vine with small green flowers. After one sniff of the putrid-smelling blossoms, I realized why it was called the carrion flower. Maybe I'd better quit while I am ahead.

I was telling my daughter-in-law Jennifer that I was anxious to try green cattails. I've read that you can cook and eat them like corn on the cob. She looked at me pityingly and said, "Alyce Faye, just because you can eat those things doesn't mean that you have to!"

I took advantage of yesterday's warmer weather to pick an early mess of greens. The dandelion greens are just right now, young and tender, with tightly curled buds almost hidden in their centers. I added a few other greens, although it is almost too early for many spring potherbs. I did find a good handful of violets (full of vitamin C) some whitetop, chickweed, a few clumps of wild potato, some springs of goosegrass (cleavers) and some narrow dock.

As I roamed over the field, I felt a deep kinship with the land, and with our grandmothers who searched the spring meadows for fresh greens to vary their winter's diet of dried and salted foods. They did it through necessity, and we do it through choice, but it is still rewarding to take advantage of nature's bounty.

Young, newly grown dock leaves can be cooked any way that you cook spinach, although many people like to combine these greens with other types of wild greens. They can also be creamed to remove the slight astringency that is objectionable to some. Cook the greens, drain and chop. For two cups of chopped greens, melt a tablespoon of butter in a saucepan, and add a tablespoon of flour. Mix thoroughly; add the greens and 1/2 cup of rich milk. Stir and cook until well mixed and slightly thickened. This can be used with any mixture of greens.

Quite possibly the most popular wild food found here is the lowly mushroom. Morels appear early in the spring. And they are so coveted by avid mushroom hunters that their "secret patches" are fiercely guarded. In a burst of generosity, Criss offered to take me to his secret "merkle" patch. I'm not sure if he took a roundabout route so I'd never find it on my own or not, but it would take a compass and a detailed map for me to find it. In any case, he has no worries—if I ever go there again, wild hogs will have to drag me. On second thought, there probably were wild hogs lurking about.

I should have been warned right in the beginning when he had to hunt for ten minutes to find a crack big enough for me to enter his wilderness. It must have been Br'er Rabbit's brier patch, for it was practically impenetrable. I don't think the foot of man had trod that patch of woods since the Indians flitted through the forest.

Criss was foraging on ahead with his eye on the ground, searching for the elusive morel. I was concentrating on clawing my way through the tangle of briers and vines that were determined to prevent my entry. Criss called back cheerily, "Are you coming along all right?"

"Oh, fine," I muttered, as I tried to detach a greenbrier from the top of my head. A multiflora rose vine grabbed me in my back, and a vicious blackberry brier wound around my legs. "Are you looking for mushrooms?" he asked accusingly. Looking for mushrooms? I was intent on survival. I couldn't have picked one if a morel as big as a gallon jug had suddenly sprouted at my feet.

He spotted a little clearing about two feet wide and four feet long. "You can look in there where it is clear," he offered. I just wondered if it were big enough to lie down and die in. My arms were bleeding, my legs were scratched and torn, and one pesky brier had punctured the end of my nose. I finally spotted a way out and gladly left his secret merkle patch for good.

When we were kids, we sampled almost everything in the woods. We roamed all over the hills and fields, tasting everything within our reach. We ate mountain tea leaves and the spicy red berries, chewed sweet birch bark, nibbled on tender sassafras shoots and spicewood twigs. We would strip the inner bark from the slippery elm tree and chew the gooey mass. (By the way, this is an excellent sore throat remedy.) I can't remember eating anything that hurt us.

This may not be classed as a wild food (or drink) but most country boys at one time or another try their hand at making homemade wine. My youngest brother, Ronnie, was no exception. Knowing Mom's reaction would be nothing short of violent he hid the end product under the hay in the old barn.

For some reason, Mom was poking around the hay when she noticed a jug sticking out through the cover of the hay. Further investigation pointed to the fact that

Ronnie had sneaked some of her canned blackberries out of the cellar.

After sniffing the contents to make sure, Mom poured the whole jug of contraband liquid on the ground, and then carefully filled the jug with water from the cattle pond. She then squeezed enough pokeberries in it to color it richly, hid it back under the hay, and went innocently to the house. My brother never mentioned the wine, but I have always wondered at his reaction when he had his first wine tasting party.

Grandpa O'Dell found a churn of home brew that his boys were making from blackberries (years ago, of course) right in the middle of the fermenting stage. He poured it in the hog trough, and the hogs guzzled it and got roaring drunk. I can hear Grandpa telling it now, slapping his leg and laughing. "Them hogs went plumb wild," he wheezed. "They ran around the pen, squealin' and staggerin', then they would fall down and waller in the mud. Come to think of it, there's not too much difference in hogs and men at times."

There is a wild foods tea that is the elixir of the gods. I am talking about sassafras tea, that springtime mountain tonic that cures the winter doldrums. To me, it is the very essence of springtime. The roots are dug, usually in February, when the ground thaws out and it is easy to dig. The bigger roots make the reddest tea.

Yes, leave the bark on the root, but scrub well with a

stiff brush to remove all the soil. Put a few pieces in a large kettle, and boil until the tea becomes red and fragrant. Keep adding water until the tea is as strong as you like. Keep your sulphur and molasses; I'll take my spring tonic in sassafras tea any time.

Animal Life in the Hills

Adrian is nine, but small for his age. His bosom pal is Cousin Joseph, who is a year younger. They are planning to catch enough wild animals to form their own zoo, and have set traps for chipmunks. Last Saturday, some of the older grandsons were helping trim weeds while their grandfather mowed. Aaron uncovered a water snake in the ditch beside the yard, which he promptly dispatched. Water snakes are quite common here and no cause for alarm.

Joseph and Adrian watched, and then went on down the creek to play. In a few minutes, they were back with a snake stuffed in a quart jar. Their grandfather didn't pay too much attention to it, thinking it was another water snake.

Aaron poured it out on the blacktop driveway and yelled at me, "Mommaw, you better come look at this—I don't think it is a water snake." It wasn't. It was a fair-sized copperhead with a blunt tail and flat head. After Criss recovered from shock, he asked Adrian, "How in the world did you get that snake in the jar?"

Adrian shrugged and said in an offhand manner, "Oh, I just stuck the jar over his head and poked him in with a stick!" Every time I think of his little stubby fingers around that snake's head, I get the shivers.

In recounting this to Mom, I remarked, "He must have a guardian angel." "Of course, they all have." She answered. "How else would they survive?" I think Adrian's guardian angel must work overtime to keep up with him.

⋅→══◉◉══←⋅

Adrian is coming along with his animal collection. He has two baby chicks of his own that a neighbor gave him, and he cares for them tenderly. He put them in a chicken coop the first night, and early the next morning his mother could see some type of furry animal in the coop with them.

Hurrying out in the yard, she was sure that it was a big cat and with a sinking heart she knew the baby chickens were gone. As she got closer, she realized it was some other animal and picked up a stick to wreak vengeance on it. She lifted up an old shaggy wig and two warm babies hopped out. Adrian thought it would make a good substitute mother, and it did.

⋅→══◉◉══←⋅

Probably the most lovable pet we ever had was a rabbit named Rosa-Belle. Actually, she belonged to Patty's boys, but we all loved her. When she first joined Patty's family, she was a fist-sized ball of gray hair. She was a guest in my house when she came to visit. She was given to Adrian a week or so before Easter, and lost no time in becoming an established member of their household.

Patty was told that you could train a rabbit to a litter box as easily as you do a kitten. From the very beginning, Rosa-Belle was faithful to her portable john. When she was here, I would put her litter box in my bathroom. It was somewhat of a shock to rush in my bathroom and find it already occupied by a tiny gray bunny looking reproachful at the invasion of her privacy.

She looked like a wild rabbit, but a tamer bunny never hopped around. We gave her the run of the house during the day. As she loved to be petted, she was constantly underfoot. I learned to walk in a queer, sliding shuffle to avoid squashing her, and even at that, I would sometimes send her scooting with the side of my foot.

She was always overjoyed to see me early in the morning when I got up to prepare breakfast. I would loose her from her prison and offer lettuce, broccoli, or raw apple. She would sniff and nibble for a few minutes, and then she was back under my feet. I would realize that she wanted to be held and petted.

She almost seemed to purr when I would pick her up and hold her close, smoothing her silky fur and caressing her ears. She especially liked to have her tummy rubbed, so I would lay her on her back and rub her down. She would respond affectionately by licking my hands, her little tongue flicking out quickly.

When Patty first brought her to our house, I fed her conventional rabbit food, supplemented by fresh vegetables and leafy goodies from the kitchen. One day for our mealtime, I baked chuck wagon beans—baked beans with hamburger and lots of spices. Patty said, "Let me show you what she really likes," and proceeded to scoop out a spoonful of beans and placed them on a napkin for the bonnie wee bunny.

Rosa-Belle took one sniff, almost visibly closed her

eyes in ecstasy, and plowed into them with gusto. "You'll kill her!" I yelled. Patty replied, "You don't know what she eats. She loves Puerto Rican beans and rice (a dish Patty makes highly seasoned with special spices) and she adores sausage, grits and eggs. . . "She'll die of high cholesterol," I warned.

Still, I found myself sneaking her tidbits of things I thought she would like. She was partial to a warm biscuit, and liked it even better if it had been sopped in gravy. Her ears were attuned to the sound of the refrigerator door opening, as she learned early that the crispers contained fresh vegetables. She would come running at the sound of the microwave oven, as we used it to take the chill off vegetables straight from the refrigerator. Rosa-Belle was hard to resist when she begged; standing erect on her hind feet with her ridiculously tiny front paws in a gesture of supplication.

She napped a lot during the day, stretched out near a furnace vent. Late in the evening, she would emerge for a romp. She would twist, leap and turn, kicking her heels straight up in the air. Daddy used the expression "quick as a cat." If he could have seen Rosa-Belle, I'm sure he would have changed it to "quick as a rabbit." She would dart at one of us, then wheel and run as if taunting us to join her in a bunny highland fling. She probably wondered why we didn't.

She did have her faults. She discovered the bookcase, and liked nothing better than shredding the dust covers on the books. Someone chewed the wallpaper in my bathroom, and although I am not accusing her, it was about bunny high. We corrected her with a rolled-up newspaper, but she would still sneak a nibble when she got a chance.

Adrian adored her, but he also liked money. When his brother Luke offered to buy her, he agreed to sell her. Patty was shocked. "Adrian," she asked in disbelief, "Would you sell your Rosa-Belle that you love so much?" A trifle shamefaced, he admitted that he would.

Luke jumped at the chance. "How much would you take for her?" he asked. "Five dollars," Adrian answered firmly—which was her original cost. Luke was indignant. "No way!" he yelled loudly. "That's a used rabbit! I'll give you $4.50!"

Yes, she was used and loved.

She got so big that they made her a pen outside, but she wouldn't stay in it. Patty was sure she was getting out at night and joining the wild rabbits that gathered nightly in the yard to frolic and romp. After she disappeared, we wondered if she had eloped with one of her wild friends and was busy making a home somewhere. We still miss her.

Matthew has always loved baby animals. Criss once had to discourage him from bringing home a bevy of skunks. He put three duck eggs in an incubator, but only one of them hatched. One night, long after Criss had gone to dreamland, Matthew called long distance to tell us his duck egg was hatching. Criss was as calm as anyone who has gone through the throes of fatherhood and grand-fatherhood many times. "Leave him alone, Matthew, and let him hatch out on his own," he advised. "They have to eat the membrane inside the eggshell before they can kick their way out." After a series of congratulations and best wishes, we settled back down to sleep.

The next day Matthew called again. "He made it!" he informed me. "I had to perform a C-section on him—now I feel like a father!" I have read that incubated chicks or ducks form a bond with the first human who takes care of them, and it must be true. That tiny scrap of fuzzy yellow and black down follows Matthew so closely that if he takes a step backward he is in danger of being tromped.

It is comical to see him get temporarily separated from his mother (father?) and crane his neck with an excited "peep." Matthew answers with a shrill "peep-peep-peep" and the little fellow runs straight as an arrow to him; his absurdly tiny wings stuck out like the fins on a fish. I "duck-sat" him last week while Matthew was camping, and dogged if I am not beginning to feel like a grandmother!

Last Friday one of the men at work brought me a baby groundhog whose mother had been killed on the road, and I carried him proudly to show Tammy, Matthew' wife. Matthew was walking down the road with his baby duck following him, and Tammy was pulling in the driveway on her way home from work.

We met at the bridge, and when Tammy got out of the car, she had a box containing a naked baby sparrow that had fallen out of a nest and Matthew had rescued. She had taken it to work with her to feed every hour or so. Matthew also has a full grown white duck that literally hates water. He introduced Gus to the pond, and the duck refused to have anything to do with that scary water. Matthew finally threw him into the pond, and he swam back panic-stricken and crouched down upon Matthew's shoes, peeping piteously.

Poor Tammy! She has a cat and a couple of kittens, two hunting dogs and a beagle pup. The puppy carries the kittens around and brings them back when they venture too near the edge of the porch. Now, besides the water-hating duck she has the baby duckling that thinks he is a person. Or perhaps he thinks Tammy and Matthew are ducks. To top it all, he brought home a half-grown rabbit that he purchased at the feed store this week. I wonder if we have missed our calling—we should have built a zoo.

⋆⟾⟾⋆

For a year or so I have begged for a cat, but Criss was happy without one. We had owned (does anyone own a cat?) yard cats and barn cats, but never a house cat. All of our cats had simply drifted here, but I had never deliberately chosen one.

My daughter-in-law's sister had a mother cat that was expecting kittens, so I told Jennifer to pick one out for me. He arrived on my birthday; a soft, striped tabby cat with lots of pure white on is tummy. He came complete with his litter box (at six weeks he was housebroken) and a fleecy cat bed—a gift from Jennifer.

Criss was a little perturbed at having a kitten in the house, and Mom was scandalized. I keep him confined in a bedroom at night, lest he take a notion to get in bed with Mom. She would probably take up her hospital bed and walk.

We had him neutered at six months, and when we brought him back from the animal hospital, we let him out of the cat carrier in the living room. He shook his head in a dazed fashion, and then to our delight, promptly turned a somersault.

He followed me out on the kitchen porch one morning, where a group of banties occupied a favorite spot beneath the snowball bush. He had never seen a chicken, and of course they had never encountered a cat. He took one startled look, arched his back, and the hair stood up on him. The banties in turn stopped dead in their tracks and eyed him.

The banties stared with beady, unblinking eyes, and he lowered his stance and crouched like a tiger after his prey. The rooster made one step toward him, and Chester turned tail and ran. I found him hiding behind the trash can as the rooster crowed triumphantly.

Late this summer, our daughter-in-law Jennifer rescued a small kitten that was destined to be destroyed. He stayed one day with her, then decided he liked my back porch better. Reuben was thrilled with him and promptly lay claim. "I'll call you Rascal," he announced, as our feline circle enlarged.

Rascal is a playful black and white cat, but he is a glutton. The first time I fed him, I poured out a pan full of cat food for all the resident cats. Jennifer's cat, Oliver, had come down for a snack and he was patiently waiting. Rascal spread his whole body over the pan of food and refused to share a morsel.

Oliver is a gentlemanly cat, and he watched the young upstart for a few minutes. Then he raised his paw and gave Rascal a healthy swat on the top of his head. It didn't faze Rascal—he kept on eating.

Our border collie, Tudor, loves to play ball. He will catch and bring the ball back as long as anyone plays with him. I heard Andy yell one day, "Hey, Tudor is picking the green tomatoes!" I guess he thought he'd found a whole field of green balls.

Life moves along in our holler; the gardens are beginning to produce abundantly, and so are our farm animals. Our neighbor Chester (not our cat) has a flock of baby chickens, and he called to inquire how to tell the sex of them. After they are a few weeks old, Criss goes by their combs. A rooster's comb is bigger than a pullet's.

Feed-store Freddie had a different method. He told our daughter Patty to lay the newly hatched chicks on their backs, and if they stuck one foot up in the air; they were roosters. I can't remember what they did if they were pullets—probably rolled over and ran.

Our neighbor Gerald once had a cow that was half Holstein and half Guernsey that sported a wicked set of horns. I don't think she was a rogue, but one day she managed to get her horns fastened in a ten-foot wooden gate. She tore the whole thing off the hinges and ran out through the pasture field with it on her head.

Old Pat, their work horse, looked up and saw this apparition coming at him with a ten-foot rack on her head, bolted, and headed for the wide open spaces. I guess he thought the Martians had landed for sure.

We raised a roan Durham bull once from a little calf, and Criss made the mistake of petting him. We kept him in a lot that included the fish pond, and Criss fed him grain from a coffee can. He was a playful pet, but when the boys would go fishing at the pond and carry their can of worms past him, he thought it ought to contain grain. He would stomp and snort because they didn't feed him, and Criss explained, "Aw, he just wants to play!" Who wants to play with a 1,500-pound bull?

Later we put him in Gerald's pasture, and one day he got out and came in their yard. For some reason, Jeff's swing set enraged him and he attacked it. It was a one-sided duel until Jeff's mother got in on the act and ran him off with a broom. Eventually, we had to sell him—he was just too much bull for us.

We have always had a close relationship with wildlife, as well as the domestic farm animals. We raised a red-tailed hawk one time (the bird was never confined, so please don't issue any citations). Henry was free to fly, but would come in a couple of times a day for a handout. We started out catching minnows for him, but that proved to be a bigger task than we could handle.

We then fed him raw deer meat, which he devoured. One day Criss yelled at me that Henry was trying to catch my kitten. It really looked that way. But what he was really doing was teasing the kitten by buzzing him. He would keep it up, flying lower and lower over its head, until the cat ran away in terror.

Criss had a coon dog that was chained to a doghouse in the edge of the yard, and this hawk was full of mischief. He knew exactly how close he could get to the dog without harm. And he would light and stamp his feet until the dog would reach the end of his chain and go wild with furious barking. You could almost see Henry laughing.

The hawk came back for a long time, catching his snack of raw venison in midair. He finally reverted completely to the wild. Many times yet today, when I see a hawk sailing serenely in the air, I wonder if it could be our Henry.

An agitated, raucous squawking came from the vicinity of the maple tree in our backyard and repeated over and over until we felt the need to investigate. Puny Pup was resting on the grass beneath the tree, staring in puzzlement at a pair of robins that flew back and forth above her.

As they began buzzing closer to her head, she got up in disgust and trotted back up the road to the safety of her own yard. It was then we realized that the parent birds were teaching their fledglings to fly, and wanted no part of a curious puppy in the vicinity.

Criss's banties are multiplying day by day. One of the hens "stole her nest out," and was out of sight for several days. She brought her babies in last week and was hovering over her little ones when Criss found her.

She was sitting quietly on her chicks when he reached down to pick her up off the doodies. Without warning, she flew into a fury of ruffled feather, claws and beak. She flogged him unmercifully until he retreated, and then she chased him halfway through the chicken lot. I don't think we will have to worry about any varmint harming her babies.

The setting hen is weaning her chicks, and our turkey Homer ended up with them. It is amusing to watch a mother hen wean her little ones. She will hide in the woods or brush, and her brood of young ones will peep frantically and search desperately for her. She knows when it is time for them to make it on their own, and continues to evade them.

When this first happened, Homer was very perturbed. He ran around the young chickens, making his peculiar perking sound. Very soon, they were following him. He seemed a little perplexed at first, as if he didn't quite know what to do with this flock of adopted stepchildren. The chickens are half grown now, and they still follow Homer. He is quite protective of them, and will threaten dog or kitten that makes a move toward his "children."

We have a rooster that hates Homer. Whether he thinks Homer has usurped his place as "cock of the walk" or it's merely masculine jealousy, we don't know. Although Homer is four times his size, he never misses a chance to attack this peace-loving turkey. Of course Homer has to defend himself, and the battle is raging.

This morning, Homer was missing. All summer, he had

suffered at the hands (feet?) of our rooster, who spurred and chased him all over the place. One day this week, Homer turned on the rooster. Kevin came rushing in the house to tell me the two were fighting and he couldn't separate them.

I grabbed Homer and held him (did you ever try holding 30 pounds of mad turkey?) while Kevin chased the rooster away. At least five times that day I had to take Homer off the rooster and rescue him. Poor rooster—Homer not only wanted to whip him, he was bent on killing him. The rooster lost a spur, part of his comb, and most of his dignity.

Finally, I shut the turkey up in the chicken house to separate them. Early the next morning, without a backward glance, Homer disappeared. Sarah said that very early, just about dawn, she thought she heard another turkey calling up in the woods. I'd like to think that Homer found a young bride and is living in a state of bliss—with a flock of young turkeys following him around.

Our family loves all animals except snakes. Mom in particular is "snaky." She grew up on Big Laurel Creek where copperheads abounded. We were camping on Williams River one time, when she almost squatted down on a big rattlesnake. She panicked (who wouldn't!) and ran through a blackberry thicket, returning to camp with her arms and legs in bloody tatters. We thought a wild animal had attacked her; I don't think the snake could have done as much damage.

When we were living out at the old Jackson County farm, Mom and Dad came up to help us hoe corn. A sudden summer shower came up while they were in the cornfield, and they sought shelter in the old log barn. Daddy picked up a Karo syrup can and handed it to Mom. As she took it, a large but harmless cow snake poked his head up, looked inquisitively at Mom and began to unwind.

With a shriek to chill the blood, she flung the can down, cleared a four-foot high window with a single bound (Superman could have done no better!) and ran to the house through the rain. I don't think she hoed any more corn that day.

Criss is almost as bad as Mom was—he has a paranoid fear of the slithery creatures. He has a truck driver, Buck, who is worse. One day last week the paving crew was waiting for a load of asphalt, and lunch hour was upon them. They decided to take advantage of the lull to eat lunch. The boys all piled up in the back of the pickup and drove to a nearby fast food restaurant, leaving Bruce, the roller man, to watch for the asphalt truck.

As they drove back to the job site, Bruce was standing beside the road with a large potato chip bag in his hand. As the truck stopped, he threw the bag in the back with the men. You would not believe that a crew of men could abandon a vehicle so fast. Buck bailed out and landed on the hard ground on his back, and the others were close behind. The poor snake was only trying to get away.

The sliding glass window was open on the cab, and Criss said if the snake had come through, Ford Motor Company would have found out if their product could really climb a tree. I don't really believe that the snake was 12 feet long and as big around as a roll of bologna, but Bruce did lay low the rest of the day.

It seems that I have broken a federal law by rescuing a little bird a few weeks ago. I didn't "bring it in," but put it in a box in the garage to protect it from predatory animals such as the one that had injured it. It was free to fly away at any time, but it couldn't fly. This was not a baby bird, but a mature female.

Still, I didn't have a federal permit to "treat" it—the only thing I did was provide food and water in case it did recover. My grandson Reuben is an accessory to the crime; in fact, he was the one who brought it to me. I would much rather my 12-year-old grandson would feel compassion for an injured bird than be one of those teenage punks with a BB gun who runs around shooting at everything that flies.

Well, if it is off to jail that Reuben and I must go, I will go without protest. However, they must take my 88-year-old mother also, as she requires the 24-hour care that I provide. Also, we must also take her wheelchair, walker, potty-chair, extended toilet seat, bath chair and hospital bed. Perhaps we can get a family room.

My sister Susie's granddaughter is also in trouble. Lyndsey looks like a miniature angel, with a mop of black curls and dark blue eyes—but appearances can be deceiving.

Seems that her parents, John and Monica found a nest of baby birds at their home. They were devoid of feathers;

just innocent, naked little birds. Lyndsey took the baby birds out of their nest and dressed them in Barbie doll clothes. (She thought they were cold.)

When Monica discovered her, she explained very firmly that handling the baby birds would cause the mother bird to desert them, and they would die. They undressed the poor creatures and put them back in the nest. The mother bird not only came back and claimed them, but also raised them to maturity until they feathered out and flew away.

Now Lyndsey did not have a federal permit to do this, so she may be joining us in the pokey. She will not go quietly, however, but kicking and screaming all the way. It could be like "The Ransom of Red Chief"—the feds may pay John and Monica to take her back.

The Great Outdoors

It is wonderful that God gave us memories to retain all of the good old times in our minds. I was telling grandson Reuben of how my Dad used to take us camping up on Hickory Knob every fall—of how we slept in a tent and cooked over an open fire—of how he would cut a grapevine for us to swing on . . . He listened intently, then inquired, "Mommaw, how do you remember all these things?" I answered jokingly, "Oh, I've got a mind like a steel trap!" He pondered for a few minutes, then said, "I have to sort out all my remembers!"

Our family has always enjoyed outings together, and whenever autumn spreads her vivid colors in the woods, we have to go camping. One year we camped out for a few days near the Ha'nted Lick, and the sugar maples dropped yellow leaves all over our camp in a deep layer of pure gold. The air was warm and fragrant with that particular perfume that Hickory Knob wears—a mixture of rich earth, hot sunshine on dry leaves, clear, clean water, and warm pine needles.

Reuben, my faithful shadow, and I stepped outside into

a delightful world of warm sunshine and blue skies this morning. The sweet clover smell of fresh-cut grass hung in the air, and the sky was deep blue and cloudless. I turned to Reuben and said, "Oh, what a beautiful day!" "Yeah," he replied enthusiastically, "It makes you swell up, don't it?"

Dreamy midsummer days float by as soft as a butterfly lighting upon a milkweed blossom. Orange butterfly weed and mauve milkweed blossoms invite congregations of black and yellow swallowtail butterflies to come and dine. Black-eyed susans stare boldly at fields of orange daylilies.

Life is good in the hills, and it is a wonderful place for our children to run free. Sometimes, though, the sharper side of life appears, and the young ones are confronted with the hard facts of life and death.

Our youngest son, Matthew, purchased some baby ducks for his three little daughters. There is a small creek running through his yard, and the baby ducks and the little girls had a great time splashing and playing in the water. One evening they returned late from the garden to find that evil had invaded their Garden of Eden. Their baby ducks were lying slaughtered on the ground, victims of a stray dog.

Sometime later I received an agonized phone call. It was Rachel, age six. And she was sobbing until I could hardly understand her. "Oh, Mommaw," she wailed. "An old dog or something has killed our baby ducks!"

I tried to console her, and asked if they had performed a proper funeral. "Yes," she answered. "We had to bury them in a double grave." I questioned her about the funeral service, and she said that Megan, age two, wanted to sing "Happy Birthday," so they did.

I tried to comfort her by telling her how happy their babies would be in duck heaven. Then four-year-old Judy called me. She too was crying and told me she didn't want her baby duck to be an angel. I said, "Think how happy your little duck is, floating around on a cloud up in the sky." "Yes, but I can't see it," she sobbed.

Their mother Tammy told me later that they grieved all day over their baby ducks. Rachel composed a letter saying, "Dear Kirby and Angel: "We love you and miss you, and we'll meet you someday in heaven." She then requested that she be buried beside her ducks.

And so life, with its joys and tragedies, goes on in the hills.

The sunsets this month have been spectacular. I have been trying to capture some of these on film, but it changes so rapidly from moment to moment that it's almost impossible.

Yesterday evening, when the first glow of red appeared in the sky, I grabbed the camera and Reuben, my four-year-old grandson who is always at my heels—and stuffed them both in the truck. When we got to the top of the hills, there was a glorious panorama spread out before our eyes.

The peaked hills were sharply etched in black against the brick red sky, and even as we watched, gray cloud tendrils streaked a sooty finger through the red. Reuben took a deep breath and said softly, "Oooh, I love it! I'd like to take a spoon and scoop it up!"

Reuben has developed a real appreciation for the things of nature, and often calls to me to "Come, look!" Sometimes it is a wildflower blooming on the bank or a butterfly floating above the flowerbed. Yesterday it was the brilliant purple of a weed stem, bereft of leaves, but a thing of beauty to him. I feel that the heritage that my father left—the deep love for God's creation—lives on in his great-grandchild.

⊶⟾⊜⟾⊷

Rueben has always helped me with my gardening chores, and while we were digging through the topsoil to plant flowers, he informed me seriously, "Mommaw, don't dig over here, or over here, or over here. I've got gold buried in them places." It makes me wonder what he does have buried.

I tried to give him a handful of change that he found on the dresser the other day, and he told me, "You don't have to give me that. I'm rich; I really am." I must have looked surprised for he added, "I'm not kidding; I am."

So am I, Reuben—I'm rich in dandelion gold and drunk with apple blossom perfume. The warm air is full of birdsong, and the earth is full of the newness of life. It is a miracle how the first spring days can dim the memory of a harsh, rigorous winter.

I am blessed in having Reuben this spring, as he will start to kindergarten this fall. He was at my heels while I was digging a flowerbed last week, and I accidentally chopped a small earthworm in two pieces. "Stop!" he yelled, and tenderly rescued the hapless worm. I went on digging and heard him say sadly, "I'm worried about this little worm—he's not going anywhere." (No wonder, he was cut in two.)

In a few minutes he shouted "Stop!" again. This time it was an ant, which he captured before the hoe hit it. Something tells me it is going to take a long time to make my flowerbeds this spring.

⟡═◦═⟡

We have always loved camping on Williams River. It is most beautiful in the springtime, after the sunshine has dried up the mud and coaxed out the wildflowers. Through the rich, dark loam of the mountain soil, a large variety of trilliums bloom. There are large purple ones, looking regal and aloof above the more modest spring beauties. Pure white ones, called the large-flowered trillium, gleam chastely among the dry, brown leaves covering the forest floor.

Smaller red trilliums, also called toadshade, are scattered all around; near the river are patches of the delicate painted trillium, a white flower with a patch of pink in the center. There are trout lilies, sometimes called dogtooth violets, which raise solitary yellow heads above brownish, mottled leaves beneath.

There are slender-stalked wood anemones, or windflowers, growing low on the ground with their white and delicate pink blooms that tremble in the wind. A multitude of yellow coltsfoot throngs both sides of the road. No wonder West Virginia is almost heaven.

⟡═◦═⟡

On the wings of a cold North wind, winter weather was

carried into our hills one night, sending birds and wild creatures alike scurrying for shelter. The brown landscape is covered with a white, icy coating, and while the creek is still running, the edges are beginning to freeze. Overhanging twigs create ice bells that dangle in the water, and mild winter days are now a memory.

As I watch my grandchildren play in the snow, it reminds me of the bobsled that Harold "Preach" Bullard made one year. We had a beautiful, deep snowstorm that closed school, and we took advantage of the unexpected holiday to play in the snow. We didn't have a lot of fancy sleighs like children do nowadays, so we would slide on anything we could find. Pieces of old linoleum were ideal.

We looked out and saw Preach coming up the road with a boxlike contraption trailing behind him. When he reached our yard, he was grinning from ear to ear. He told us, "I've made a sled big enough for all of us to ride on." It was big. Despite all our efforts, pushing and pulling, we couldn't get the sled more than three or four feet up the hill. Dejected, Preach turned and pulled the sled back down the road to his house.

I wonder what happened to it. It would have made an excellent bomb shelter, or a launching pad for a rocket to the moon. One thing for sure, it is undoubtedly still around.

My baby sister Susie and her friends once utilized a car hood as a sled. A whole gang of kids piled on it and rode it down the church hill. Of course it couldn't be steered, and it veered off the road and took down over the side of the steep hill. Marie Hopkins raised her head up to view her surroundings just as a gas line stretching across a gully loomed in their path.

Everyone ducked their heads as the car hood slid beneath the pipe—except Marie, who didn't respond fast enough. The pipe caught her on the top of her head and knocked her out cold. I don't think they tried that any more. I wonder why I worry when my grandkids slide off the bank behind their house.

Remember how we used to play "Fox and Geese" when we got a deep snow? We would trample out a huge circle in the snow, with paths like spokes in a wheel inside the circle. The designated fox would stand in the center of the circle, with the geese running around the outside rim. The fox would dart up and down the paths, hoping to snag a laggardly goose which in turn became the fox. You never see kids playing this now. They are too busy watching TV or playing computer games.

About this time of year, when our spirits seemed to be drooping, we felt that "spring's just around the corner"— but it's a long corner indeed, Daddy would cheer us up with his annual pep talk. "Spring will come," he would say, "and the wind will blow and dry up the mud. The sun will peep out and shine warm, and the green grass will grow. The flowers will bloom, and the birds will build nests. The ground will get warm, and you can take off your shoes and go barefoot."

We would listen, entranced, and could hardly wait until spring was here. I was repeating this litany to three-year-old Rachel, who was as enchanted by it as we used to be. About halfway through my recital, the sun suddenly shone through the skylight. And she threw her arms wide and shouted, "It's here!"

Mountain Poetry

Our people sometimes try their hand at composing poems, and my sister Susie is a prime example of a frustrated poet. (Actually, she does pretty good.) She composed this one after her son Noel had a motorcycle wreck—not serious.

This is the bike that Noel spilt.
This is the cat that lay by the bike that Noel spilt.
This is the dog that chased the cat that lay
  by the bike that Noel spilt.
This is the bike with the blaring horn that worried
  the dog that chased the cat that lay by the bike
  that Noel spilt.
This is the maiden all aglow, that waited for Noel
  to put on a show,
As he stood the bike up on its toe, that worried
  the dog that chased the cat that lay by the bike
  that Noel spilt.
This is the boy all forlorn that hated the maiden
  for her scorn,
Who wrecked the bike and crumpled its horn,
Who kicked the dog and stomped the cat, that lay
  by the bike that Noel spilt.

(Original poem by Susie Braley Loomis)

She also composed one for our son Mike, who bought a big motorcycle and proceeded to show off for us. He was riding up the paved road, when Susie yelled, "Pop a wheelie, Mikie!" So he did. He rode the bike for a few seconds, and then the bike rode him.

> *There was a boy named Michael,*
> *Who went up the road on his 'cycle*
> *When a wheelie he popped,*
> *And over he flopped.*
> *And now Mike's riding his tricycle.*

Susie wrote this one right after Christmas several years ago. I think it is one of her best.

THE DAY AFTER CHRISTMAS

> *'Twas the day after Christmas*
> *When all through the home,*
> *The turkey was carved,*
> *Clear down to the bone.*
>
> *The stockings were flung*
> *Almost everywhere,*
> *The house was a mess,*
> *The larder was bare.*
>
> *The children were romping*
> *Upon every bed,*

They won't mind a thing
This vacation I dread.

I'm still in my duster,
Dad's taking a nap,
Wish I had some tea,
But I don't have a drap.

When away in the bedroom,
There arose such a clatter,
I ran through the hall
Screaming, "What is the matter?"

"You miserable varmints,
Your heads I will bash,
If you keep up this fighting,
I'll give you a lash!"

As I looked out the window,
It was starting to snow,
And I was trying to step
Over objects below.

When what to my wondering
Eyes should appear,
But a big white car
Pull up in the rear.

With a little old driver,
So lively and quick

I knew in a moment,
It was my Uncle Dick.

More rapid than vultures,
My cousins they came
And he hollered and shouted,
And called them by name.

"Now Mabel and Gertie,
Now Buford and Huey,
On Rufus, on Isabel,
On Elbert and Louis."

"Let's rush to the porch,
The snow's starting to fall,
Now dash away dash away,
Dash away all."

They ran through the house,
After mumbling "Hi"
Followed in by their dogs,
And a cat that's nearby.

I tried to ignore them.
But I heard them repeat,
"Oh please, won't you tell us
What is there to eat?"

As I gritted my teeth
And gave them a frown,

They told me the news
That was sure to astound.

"We've come for a spell.
I know you won't mind,
Since I've lost my job.
We've got far behind."

"We've spent all our food stamps,
And ran out of wood,
So we've come here to stay,
I think that we should."

"And is dinner ready?
I'd like rolls and jelly,
Some ham and potatoes,
To put in my belly."

"Do you have any cake?
Or pie on the shelf?"
I started to weep,
In spite of myself.

"How about some chicken,
And hot, homemade bread,
Some chocolate candy,
Or fancy cheese spread?"

My lips started trembling,
My hands started to shake,

I said to myself,
"This I cannot take."

I said not a word,
But went straight to my purse,
I reached for my car keys,
Then turned with a jerk.

I ran out the door,
As fast as a ha'nt.
When I reached the car,
I was starting to pant.

I started the engine,
It let out a roar,
When I saw some people
Rushing out the door.

I threw up my hand,
As I drove out of sight,
"Have a lovely time,
I'm leaving tonight!"

My cousin Frank "Bobby" Samples was quite talented in composing poetry, and in keeping with the season he recently wrote this:

Here I sit, short-winded, full of turkey and ham.
Stuffed to the gills—that's what I am.
Wishing I'd let a few things pass by

Like that chocolate cake and rich pecan pie.
So I guess I have cause to find a solution
With a recycled old New Year's resolution.
But it seems of my gluttony, there is no end
And the next holiday, I'll do it again.

Here is another one of his, with a lesson in it.

BROWN BIRD

I used to hunt birds in my boyhood,
Robins and sparrows and wren,
I hunted them up on the mountains,
I hunted them down in the glen.

One day when I was out hunting
I spied a brown bird on a tree,
Merrily whistling and chirping
And happy as a brown bird could be.

I lifted my gun and I fired,
The course of the bullet was true.
For a moment the little thing fluttered,
Then off to the bushes it flew.

I followed it quickly and softly
In shame I then bowed down my head,
For close to a nest full of young ones,
It was lying there bleeding and dead.

By Frank "Bobby" Samples

⋅⊱═◉═⊰⋅

This one was written my grandson Nicholas, when he was 12. Being his grandmother, I think it is good.

SHADOW

I am on the wall
I am on the ground,
A part of you that cannot be found.
I mimic your movement
Like you in every way,
Whether in January or May.
I am lost in the evening,
Found at dawn,
And when you turn your light on.
I am your shadow,
And a little bit of you,
I'll be with you always,
In everything you do.

By Nicholas Bragg

The Passing of Time

As the evening sun slides down behind the hills and twilight shadows deepen from mauve to purple on Pilot Knob, the porch swing beckons. The creak of the swing blends with the chirping of the crickets, a fall lullaby that is soothing and peaceful. A couple of lines of an old song slip unbidden into my mind, and instantly I am transported back to another porch swing, and another time.

"Once in the dear, dead days beyond recall, when on the earth the mists begin to fall . . ." This swing is old and creaky, suspended from a rough pole in the rafters. Woodbine, now turning scarlet, winds around the porch posts and covers one end of the porch behind the swing. It makes a cozy alcove for the barefoot children who are crowded together on the old swing.

The smoke from Grandpa's pipe, as familiar as Grandpa himself, drifts through the evening air. The rocking chair squeaks as he rocks the baby and smokes his pipe. Daddy is leaning back on a straight chair, propped against the wall. The conversation is low and companionable, and blended with the chirping of the crickets it makes the sleepy little children on the swing even sleepier. Soon it will be time to gather back in the living room, for Bible reading and bedtime prayer. Ah, those were the dear, dead days.

We didn't have the foggiest idea of what the "dear, dead days" were, but it pulled at our heart strings as we sang the babies to sleep each night. Jeannie was my baby, and Mary Ellen claimed Susie. I can see those little blonde girls now, clad in their feed sack gowns, with their heads nestled on our shoulders.

We sang. "And in the dusk, where fell the firelight gleam, softly it wove itself into our dream." Although the firelight didn't gleam, the gas mantles gave out a dim, wavering light. The katydids sang their own sad song of dying summer and coming fall. Far away, the lonely hoot of an owl would sound, but we were safe and happy there on the old porch swing.

"Just a song at twilight, when the lights are low, and the flickering shadows, softly come and go. Though the heart be weary, sad the day and long, still to us at twilight, comes love's old song . . ."It is a song of love that I am hearing, Daddy's voice from long ago reading the verses of scripture that were precious to him, and now are precious to me.

I see again the children kneeling beside chairs and couch, tow-headed Mark and Ronnie, and Larry with darker hair. The girls are all blonde—Mary Ellen, Jeannie, Susie and myself. I hear the little ones saying their simple "Now I Lay Me Down to Sleep," and the older children praying, "Our Father which art in heaven." I hear the earnest tone in Daddy's voice as he thanked the Lord for all his many blessings, and entreated God to save and keep his children.

The years have passed, the old swing is gone, and the little children grew up also. Of course Grandpa, Daddy and

Mom are gone on, and the seven children are now five. We lost Mark to cancer at 56 years of age, and Ronnie passed away at 61. The memories still linger . . .

The last verse of the song goes, "Even today, we hear love's song of yore, deep in our heart it dwells forevermore. Footsteps may falter, weary grow the way, still we can hear it at the close of day. So till the end when life's dim shadows fall, love will be found the sweetest song of all."

The memories of those long ago days are still singing a song of love. Love never dies.

The children grew up, the grandchildren appeared, and now a whole batch of great-grandchildren romps through our family. These little ones are as unconsciously funny as the first group. They are so unaffected and honest. God has blessed us abundantly with 18 great-grands, so far. And it's not over yet.

When four-year-old Brionna was visiting her Aunt Patty recently, she got up one morning and crawled up on Pat's lap. "What do you want for breakfast, Bree?" Patty asked. Sleepily, she answered, "Eggs." "How do you like your eggs?" Patty asked. With enthusiasm, Brionna told her, "Oh, I like 'em a lot!"

She sounded so much like her mother Crystal when she was about the same age. The same Patty was altering some dresses for Crystal, and in pinning up a hem, she asked her, "How long do you wear your dresses, Crystal?" Crystal answered in resignation, "Oh, a lo-o-ong time!" She did too.

It is no wonder that the Bible tells us that "we spend our years as a tale that I told." Looking back, it seems such a short time ago that we swung our baby sisters in the old porch swing, and Grandpa, Mom and Daddy were here. The years passed so swiftly, and we were young mothers swinging our own babies—wasn't that just yesterday?

Now we have great-grandchildren and it is bewildering to think, where did the years go? They passed one day at a time, and we are nearing the ending of our tale. Solomon sums it up best in Ecclesiastes 12:13,14 when he says, "Let us hear the conclusion of the whole matter: Fear God, and keep his commandments: for this is the whole duty of man. For God shall bring every work into judgment, with every secret thing, whether it be good, or whether it be evil."

The generation gap between small children and older people seems to narrow as the adult grows older. Certainly there is a rapport between my mother, who is in her eighties, and her great-grandchildren that is beautiful to see. It can come as a shock to a parent, however, when they realize that their own children view them as "old."

I remember when one of my children (years ago) asked me to tell them about the "good old days when you were young." I thought then that the good old days were back in my mother's childhood.

When grandson Adrian, twelve years old, was convalescing from a fractured femur this summer, he was lying on my couch leafing through a merchandise catalog. I was shocked to hear him ask me, "Mommaw, what kind of money did they use back in your day?" Maybe he thought it was Confederate money, but Mom said it was more likely pieces of eight.

The children don't realize it, but all too soon the day in which they are now living will be the "good old days."

Time goes on, and there are the inevitable changes in the family. Daddy is gone, and so is Mom. She eventually fell and broke a hip, and we took her in our home. A year later, she broke the second hip, and Alzheimer's disease was also taking its toll. Sometimes she is like one of the little children, and we are blessed in the fact that she is sweet and easy to take care of.

A lot of the time she is dwelling in the past, but she has retained her sense of humor and always has a feisty answer for everyone. One morning I was giving her a bed bath, and we were discussing her sister Ruby who had recently died.

"What killed Ruby?" she demanded. I tried to explain that Ruby was past 90 years old, and had cancer as well. I went on to say that the Bible only gives us a life span of three score and ten years. "I'll soon be 70," I added. (Now I am 73.) She looked startled and questioned, "Am I older than you?"

Well, you are my mother, and you'd better be older than I am," I answered. She looked more disbelieving, and asked, "I'm your mother?" I tried to explain and told her, "Yes, your are my mother, and Larry's mother, and Mary Ellen's mother; you were Mark's mother, (Mark is deceased) Ronnie's mother, Jeannie's mother, and Susie's mother."

She looked at me for a minute, then retorted, "No wonder I'm so tired!" Then she flopped over on her side and went back to sleep.

This rainy weather has kept us cooped up in the house, sometimes with assorted grandkids and great-grandkids. I remarked to Mom how lonely it would be without these little ones, and she agreed. I must confess that it is rarely lonely around here.

Mike brought his two grandkids, Donovan and Alexis to visit the other day. Lexi gathered all the stuffed animals out of the toy box and piled them on Mom's lap. You could barely see Mom's face amid the toys. She loved it. She is confined to her recliner most of the time, and has a good lap to hold the little ones. We are blessed to have an extended family.

It is a joy to watch the grandchildren and great-grand-children, especially in the summertime. The Rose of Sharon bush has burst into a mass of deep pink blooms to welcome the coming of August. In the shade of this shrub, there is an odd assortment of items. Two five-gallon buckets support a wide board, while another bucket holds a smaller board and two tiny skillets, plus a large bowl.

The table is spread with bowls, cups, a pitcher of water and other items essential to a playhouse. Three little blonde girls and another one with long, dark hair preside over the stove and table, while one smaller boy (five-year-old Hunter) basks in the attention of his sisters and cousins.

Morgan, Molly, Taylor and Belinda are deeply engrossed in one of the most pleasurable joys of childhood—a homemade playhouse. Their imagination knows no bounds. It is so heartwarming to see little girls playing in this fashion, just as we did when we were young. They are practicing to become mommas and wives, and you can witness the instinctive nurturing that little girls possess in the way they treat Hunter.

We see elaborate ready-made playhouses here and there, but nothing takes the place of a cardboard box covered with a cloth, and a jelly glass of wild flowers centered on this "table." Hunter makes a trip to the kitchen door to ask, "Have you got any 'gredients to give us?"

This poem was written for Glada Vaughan by her brother, Garrett (Buster) Bragg in 1973.

TO SIS:

> *Do you remember, Sis, the days gone by?*
> *How green were the meadows, how blue the sky,*
> *And the pleasant days spent along our creek,*
> *The evening games of hide and seek,*
> *A bushel of wheat, a bushel of rye,*
> *All not ready, holler I.*
>
> *How the cat bird called from the orchard trees,*
> *The pleasant drone of the homing bees,*

The "baccer" flies in the four-o-clocks.
The vixen's bark from the ol' fox rocks,
A bushel of wheat, a bushel of kraut,
All not hid, better watch out.

How to sneak to play, our chores we'd shirk,
In the stable fields where the striped giants lurk,
The waving fields of midsummer corn,
A rooster's crow on a summer morn.
A bushel of wheat, a bushel of rye,
All not hid, holler I.

Our "tortle team" at the slick rock pool,
The long hike through the woods to school.
The scurrying squirrel in the hickory grove,
The barred owl's boom from the beechen cove,
A bushel of wheat, a bushel of corn,
I'm gonna find you, sure as you're born.

We're aging, Sis, and we can never,
Relive those days, they are gone forever.
But I've few regrets as I drift along,
That I'm nearing the end of that childhood song.
A bushel of wheat, a bushel of clover,
All not hid, can't hide over.

Afterword

Some may wonder about the children in this book Michael, our oldest, retired from Dow Chemical on April 1, 2009. His three children, Jeremy, David and Christina have produced three grandchildren.

Patty is re-married, and her three boys, Aaron, Luke and Adrian have given her a total of six grandchildren.

Two of Kevin's children, Abigail and Josh, have a total of five children, and Reuben (my sidekick) graduated from high school in 2009.

Andy has been married twice; his first family, Benji, Jessica and Joseph, have presented him with four grandchildren. Nicholas is in middle school and Taylor is in elementary.

Matthew has a total of five children, four of them girls. Rachel, Alexandria (known as Judy) Megan, and Belinda (Lynnie) make up the girls, and Jacob (Jake) came along at the last. Rachel has graduated from high school and is working; all the rest are in school.

Crystal lives in NC, where she has three little girls, Alyssa, Brionna and Mylie. She home schools them. With twelve unmarried grandchildren, we can expect great-grandchildren for years to come.

About the Author

Alyce Faye Bragg grew up and still lives in the hills of Clay County, West Virginia. She reveals her love for the country and its inhabitants in her writing, and also her deep love for God. She has written a weekly column for the *Charleston Gazette* since 1991, and also writes for the *Clay County Free Press*. She is the author of two other books, *This Holler is My Home* and *Homesick for the Hills*. She and her husband Criss are the parents of six children, 22 grandchildren, and 18 great-grandchildren.

This book spans several generations, and relates the humorous side of country living. May it be a blessing to you.